The Devil's Topographer

The Devil's Topographer

Ambrose Bierce and the American War Story

David M. Owens

The University of Tennessee Press / Knoxville

Portions of the discussion of "An Occurrence at Owl Creek Bridge" in chapter
3 originally appeared as "Bierce and Biography: The Location of Owl Creek
Bridge" in *American Literary Realism* 26, no. 3 (1994): 82–89. Reprinted
with permission.

This book is printed on acid-free paper.

Library of Congress Cataloging-in-Publication Data

Owens, David M., 1954-
The devil's topographer : Ambrose Bierce and the American war story /
David M. Owens.— 1st ed.
    p. cm.
Includes bibliographical references and index.

ISBN 1-57233-464-9

1. Bierce, Ambrose, 1842-1914?—Criticism and interpretation.
2. Bierce, Ambrose, 1842-1914?—Knowledge—Military history.
3. United States—History—Civil War, 1861-1865—Literature and the war.
4. War stories, American—History and criticism.
 I. Title.

PS1097.Z5O95 2006
813'.4—dc22   2005025946

This book is dedicated to my wife, Sandra Visser, philosopher, who chased Ambrose Bierce with me on foot, mountain bike, and four-wheel drive, and whose thoughtful reflections and insights were invaluable. It is also dedicated to our sons, Logan, who grew up with it; Sander, who will have no idea what we are talking about for several more years; and Joel, whom we pray lives to read it.

Contents

Illustrations

Preface
Defining the American War Story

> PEACE, *n*. In international affairs, a period of
> cheating between two periods of fighting.
> WAR, *n*. A by-product of the arts of peace. [. . .]
> War loves to come like a thief in the night: pro-
> fessions of eternal amity provide the night.
> BATTLE, *n*. A method of untying with the teeth a
> political knot that would not yield to the tongue.
> NOVEL, *n*. A short story padded.
>
> Ambrose Bierce
> *The Devil's Dictionary* (1911)

> Publishers want nothing from me but novels—
> and I'll die first.
>
> Bierce in a letter
> September 1903

In a brief essay written at the end of the Civil War entitled "The Real
War Will Never Get in the Books," Walt Whitman claimed that the war
"was not a quadrille in a ball-room. Its interior history will not only
never be written—its practicality, minutia of deeds and passions, will
never be even suggested" (330). Yet Whitman himself was already struggling to write a portion of that "interior history" with many of the
sketches in *Specimen Days and Collect* and with many of the poems in
Drum Taps. In the postbellum years, writers such as John William De
Forest, Ambrose Bierce, and Stephen Crane emerged who seemed willing to attempt the task of somehow fictionally representing "the minutia
of deeds and passions" of what was, until that time, America's biggest
and arguably first modern war.

War is the subject of some of the very oldest and most enduring forms
of literature. The hero of the Babylonian epic of *Gilgamesh*, the earliest
known major literary work, longs for the life of a warrior. Roughly thirteen

hundred years later, Homer set *The Iliad* against the backdrop of the Greeks' siege of the city of Troy. The Old Testament's books of history, Judges in particular, are one of the first collections to include extensive accounts of various military conflicts. Today, many universities offer courses in war literature. Selections from Tim O'Brien's writings about Vietnam are a frequent feature in widely read anthologies of American fiction. His composite novel, *The Things They Carried*, along with *Going After Cacciato* have become a part of the contemporary canon. W. W. Norton and Company even offers *The Norton Book of Modern War* among its respected anthologies. The term *war story* is one everyone seems to know and use. A frequent and informal catchall description for war literature, it is nevertheless absent from literary guidebooks and dictionaries, even one as comprehensive and voluminous as *The Penguin Dictionary of Literary Terms and Literary Theory*. In common parlance, the term gets applied to oral anecdotes and recollections of adventures, both major and minor, that typically have absolutely nothing to do with military conflict. It is a term widely used yet left largely undefined.

War story needs a precise definition. Before turning to a detailed examination of Ambrose Bierce's Civil War fiction, some consideration of this most basic terminology is necessary. Lumping works as diverse as an epic poem such as *John Brown's Body*, an autobiography such as *Personal Memoirs of U. S. Grant*, a novel such as *The Red Badge of Courage*, a play such as *The Andersonville Trial*, a poem such as "Cavalry Crossing a Ford," and a short story such as "Chickamauga" all under the general category of war stories hardly seems appropriate. Such a usage fails to discriminate, for example, among literary genres, or between what authors present as fiction and what they present as fact. To bring some precision to the term for a discussion of Bierce's work, *war story* will herein refer to a type of short fiction. More specifically, the term describes a type of short story predominantly concerned with or inherently linked to armed military conflict. Its main character or characters need not necessarily be combatants, but the conflict significantly influences their actions, affects, and fates. A war story is not necessarily set in a scene of combat; in fact, it need not take place during a time of war at all. The setting of Ernest Hemingway's "Soldier's Home," for example, is far removed from World War I Europe, but the story concerns the effects of the war on a survivor. Like most short stories, the war story typically contains the element of drama, concentrates on a single or a few characters during a relatively brief period of time, tends to focus on a single event, and moves swiftly towards a climax. Like other short stories, the war story may take the form of a tale or a frame-story, and it may be part of a story cycle or composite novel. In this discussion, the far more general term *war fiction* includes (but is not necessarily limited to) novels, novellas, short stories, tales, and sketches. The still more general term *war literature* includes both the fictional representations already mentioned as well as non-fictional texts such as histories, memoirs, and letters.

An old army joke explains the difference between a fairy tale and a war story. A fairy tale, the joke goes, always begins with "Once upon a time," but a war story always begins "This is no bullshit!" This difference highlights points essential to any discussion of war fiction and serves as an especially important springboard for a study of Ambrose Bierce. The first point is the teller's insistence on the story's authenticity. The second is a closely related one and concerns the credibility of the storyteller. Specifically, in the joke one may infer from the teller's insistence on authenticity that he appears to have been a participant in the conflict, or, at the very least, has heard the story from a trusted source who was.

As in the army joke, successful war fiction places a premium on achieving the quality of authenticity or verisimilitude. Vietnam author and former infantryman Tim O'Brien expresses this concern in the "How to Tell a True War Story" chapter of *The Things They Carried*. Claims O'Brien:

> In any war story, but especially a true one, it's difficult to separate what happened from what seemed to happen. [. . .] afterward, when you go to tell about it, there is always that surreal seemingness, which makes the story seem untrue, but which, in fact represents the hard and exact truth as it *seemed*. [. . .] it's safe to say that in a true war story nothing is ever absolutely true. [. . . but] You'd feel cheated if it never happened. Without the grounding reality, it's just a trite bit of puffery [. . .]. (78, 88–89)

Like O'Brien, Ernest Hemingway, in his introduction to the 1942 anthology *Men at War*, attempts to capture much of the essence of the war story. Hemingway explains, "A writer's job is to tell the truth. His standard of fidelity to the truth should be so high that his invention, out of his experience, should produce a truer account than anything factual can be" (xv). Here again, one of the foremost writers of war fiction is attempting to come to grips with the concern for authenticity in what is clearly presented as fiction.

As was certainly the case in the Civil War, unsuccessful war fiction tends to be nationalistic and propagandistic, frequently written during a conflict by a well-intentioned author attempting to motivate feelings of patriotism and support of the war effort. Such stories also tend to be largely forgotten because they are somehow perceived as untrue. Again, Hemingway explains:

> If, during a war, conditions are such that a writer cannot publish the truth because its publication would do harm to the State he should write and not publish. [. . .] But if he ever writes something which he knows in his inner self is not true, for no matter what patriotic motives, then he is finished. After the war the people will have none of him because he, whose obligation is to tell them the truth, has lied to them. (xv)

Both O'Brien and Hemingway wrestle with attempting to explain fiction that is somehow truer than fact. That is to say they attempt capturing the essence of the experience with a sense of authenticity that a recitation of facts alone simply fails to convey—what O'Brien calls a story that "makes the stomach believe." Clearly a central concern of war fiction is creating the impression that it could, or did, happen.

Well before Ernest Hemingway's first authorial efforts and very long before Tim O'Brien's, Ambrose Bierce began struggling to get the real war, or at least his memory of it, into the books. Many of his war stories produce a fundamental, visceral reaction from his readers that was the genesis of this study. That reaction is the simple question, "I wonder if that really happened?"

Acknowledgments

I would like to thank Chris Gavel of Hebron, Indiana, and Steve Pettus of Elkmont, Alabama, for their help with research for this book. Many thanks to those who read manuscripts, Warren Grabau, Michael W. Schaefer, G. Richard Thompson, Robert May, John N. Duvall, and especially Robert Paul (Bob) Lamb. Finally, I am very grateful to James Nagel for his encouragement and support of this project from its outset and for his extraordinary patience while attempting to teach an infantryman to write.

Introduction

Chasing Ambrose Bierce

> This is the simple story of a battle; such a tale as
> may be told by a soldier who is no writer to a
> reader who is no soldier.
>
> **Ambrose Bierce**
> "What I Saw of Shiloh" (1881)

This is a detailed examination of Ambrose Bierce's Civil War fiction. Its primary contentions are that his war stories document his own pilgrimage through the war and that thematic concerns and craft techniques in them reflect Bierce's development as a soldier much more than his growth as an artist. A secondary, closely related concern is with Bierce's place in the development of the war story itself, if not as a distinctive genre at least as something akin to one. The assertion here, discussed primarily in the preface and afterword, is that verisimilitude is the essential element of such stories and that Bierce, although not generally among the first order of American authors, is certainly a pioneer of the form.

It would be difficult to overstate the impact of his personal experience in the war on Bierce's fiction. It is in large measure responsible for his gritty, unflinching depictions of the Civil War's horrors. Biographers and literary critics alike are in virtually unanimous agreement on this point. Carey McWilliams, for example, claims that the early ideal for Bierce was the military: "the pen did not supplant the sword until he was nearly thirty. [. . .] The war was a great emotional adventure that carried Bierce from his early life on an Indiana farm deep into the darkest recesses of experience" (64). Every Bierce critic and biographer comments that the influence of Bierce's war experience strongly informs the quality of verisimilitude present in much of his best work. However, for all of its importance in Bierce's fiction there are no detailed, comprehensive, published studies of exactly how specific experiences surface in it.

H. L. Mencken, in an essay published in 1927, points out the fundamental impact of Bierce's military involvement on his fiction when he observes that Bierce "was the first writer of fiction ever to treat war realistically. He antedated even Zola. [. . .] What he got out of his services in the field was not a sentimental horror of it, but a cynical delight in it." Writing about war, says Mencken, gave the delighted cynic his greatest opportunity to demonstrate "the infinite imbecility of man" (61–62). Although the cynicism noted by Mencken is the fundamental theme underlying Bierce's war fiction as well as almost all his work, other aspects of his stories reflect the impact of his army career as well. Edmund Wilson points out that Bierce's prose style reflects a military influence. He claims that the "best qualities of Bierce's prose are military—concision, severe order and unequivocal clearness. His diction is the result of training and seems sometimes rather artificial" (631–32). Wilson is one of many critics who note that Bierce draws on personal experiences not only for what he tells, but for how he tells it as well. However, none of them pursue the point in any detail beyond reciting a few vignettes in Bierce's war memoirs that show up again as scenes in his short fiction.

Roy Morris, Jr., a historian and Bierce's most recent biographer, captures the essential Bierce more accurately than any other when, in commenting on many of the scholarly studies of Bierce's work, he states:

> Such studies, while no doubt good for the graduate schools, miss the salient point about Bierce's work, the one thing that will always differentiate him from his more talented contemporaries Mark Twain and Stephen Crane: the personal quality of his witness. When the time-worn image of Bitter Bierce [. . . is] stripped away, what finally remains is 1st Lt. Ambrose Bierce, Ninth Indiana Infantry, the bloodied veteran of Shiloh, Chickamauga, Pickett's Mill, and a dozen other battlefields who had experienced war on a scale—both large and small—that no other American writer had ever known in the half century preceding World War I. (270)

The details of "the personal quality of his witness" are the essential matter of this study. From them, several significant points emerge that illuminate how Bierce achieves that quality, and, in so doing, gives the American canon some of its most enduring war stories.

As mentioned in the preface, the I-wonder-if-that-really-happened? reaction along with O'Brien's observation that "you'd feel cheated if it never happened" is a useful starting point. Eric Solomon comments that a "remarkable aspect of Bierce's very short war stories is that in each he manages to evoke the feeling of reality, the sense of fact and place that makes war not an abstract moral condition but a concrete physical actuality" (185). The details Bierce includes about the settings in his war stories primarily convey the sense of place Solomon mentions. Daniel Aaron also emphasizes a key point about Bierce's settings: "thanks to an almost uncanny visual sense cultivated by his wartime duties as topographical engineer, he managed to fix in his mind the terrain he had traversed and to map his stories and sketches so that the reader can visualize every copse or ravine or stream he mentions" ("Ambrose Bierce" 172).

What critical approach to take and how best to organize an examination of Bierce's war stories presents basic choices. Because Bierce's Civil War fiction is such a reflection of its author's life and times, a traditional historical-biographical approach seems appropriate for a detailed study of how specific war experiences surface in his fiction and an assessment of their significance to his work. This study takes just such an approach. It is very traditional in its theoretical orientation, its methodology, and its analysis of evidence. When it compares textual evidence to the historical record, any assertions based primarily on speculation are identified as such; otherwise, the analysis and conclusions presented are supported by at least a preponderance of evidence.

This book is not an attempt to see if Bierce gets it right—that is, to argue whether or not his war stories accurately reflect the historical record and documented nonfiction accounts and studies of the behavior of Civil War soldiers in battle. Michael W. Schaefer has largely accomplished such a task very well in his 1997 work *Just What War Is: The Civil War Writings of De Forest and Bierce*.[1] Rather, this book identifies the myriad intersections of Bierce's war fiction (though certainly not all of them) with documented history as well as geography and argues for the significance of such instances.

One could arrange a study of Bierce's Civil War stories topically, as Mary Grenander does in *Ambrose Bierce*. Bierce certainly tended to revisit similar themes and motifs. One could arrange them chronologically by publication date, a technique that often offers revealing looks at the artistic development, or lack thereof, of the writer. Such an approach usefully highlights some significant observations about Bierce as an artist, the most prominent being his artistic decline immediately after the turn of the century when his writing became mostly predictable ghost stories. However, a far more revealing examination results from considering Bierce's twenty-two war stories chronologically according to the time of the action of the story, generally as editors Russell Duncan and

David J. Klooster have helpfully done in their recent anthology *Phantoms of a Blood-Stained Period*.[2] By doing so, the methodology of this study yields some surprising new insights into one of the masters of the short story. Arranging the stories in such a chronology and plotting the locations of their settings yields a reasonably accurate chart of Bierce's own progress through the war. For purposes of easy reference and summary, Appendix 1 charts Bierce's location in relation to his war stories, and Appendix 2 identifies relevant stories in relation to a time line of events in Bierce's military career. The locations are illustrated in map 1.

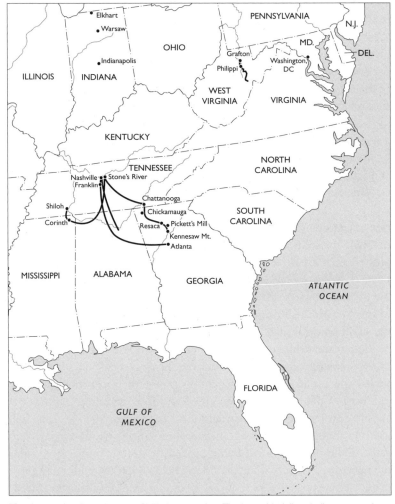

Map 1. Ambrose Bierce's major Civil War campaigns. The heavy black lines indicate general routes Bierce followed.

A simple way to determine where Bierce was from the time he assumed duties as a brigade topographer until he was wounded late in the war is to read General William Babcock Hazen's *A Narrative of Military Service*. Hazen's memoir contains fairly detailed descriptions of locations as well as maps of major engagements. Hazen and Bierce traveled together; no brigade commander would let a staff officer as valuable as the one who helped him chart the battlefield get too far away from him. Their relationship will be more fully discussed in the next chapter. Unfortunately, the Ninth Indiana Volunteer Infantry Regiment, the unit Bierce originally enlisted in, did not leave a detailed regimental history. In many cases, its location on any given day of the war can only be determined from maps, official records of higher headquarters, memoirs, and published histories of regiments that fought alongside it.

Bierce also published half a dozen short memoirs about the war. These "bits of autobiography," as Bierce was to call them in his *Collected Works*, richly inform any discussion of his war stories, so much so that critics sometimes carelessly conflate the two genres and fail to make necessary distinctions between them. The memoirs frequently highlight incidents and locales that Bierce would recast in his works of fiction. Literary studies have generally not proceeded further than this sort of cross-referencing of memoir and short story. Biographies have made use of primary documents such as letters, official records, and newspaper articles to reconstruct Bierce's life, but neither literary critics nor historians have combined these resources into a rigorous examination of exactly how Bierce's war experiences surface in his fiction. What follows does so using the stories-in-wartime-chronology arrangement. In addition to archival documents already mentioned, contemporaneous maps and personal field research retracing Bierce's steps through the war in substantially the same sequence as he took them richly inform this study.

Both the settings and incidents that Bierce borrows from life contribute to the general acclaim of his war stories as his best work. The settings he uses for these incidents, and for totally fictitious ones as well, add an unmistakable note of authenticity that some critics, attempting to classify Bierce, point to as a realistic quality of his fiction. Simply put, one pattern that emerges about Bierce's settings is that his habit was to write about places as they were when he saw them, regardless of whether the events of the story are based on real incidents or purely invented. In itself, this is not particularly remarkable except that it includes a temporal element as well. That is to say, Bierce always casts the action of his war stories during the same time period that he was at the place or places he writes about. Although Bierce was always faithful to the larger historical context of the war, he makes frequent modifications to the actual geography of the settings—a fact that might surprise some given that the bulk of his war experience was as a mapmaker, a position that made him intimately familiar with the terrain. These topographic twists are never wholly fictional, nor are they entirely factual. More often, they are a composite of existing natural features and man-made structures.

Two other general patterns emerge as well. The first is that when Bierce tells a war story that deals with the human psyche under extraordinary stress, he tends to do so in a setting that is only vaguely identifiable or that is a fictional composite of features from different locations. The second is that when Bierce tells a story with supernatural elements, he sets it in a very specific, identifiable location. The quality of verisimilitude so prominent in these stories results not from "pure" realism, but from an often complex blending of the real with the imaginary, which is an aesthetic grounded in the romance and later prominent in naturalism and modernism. Moreover, and most significantly, his stories document his own pilgrimage through the war, and thematic concerns in them reflect Bierce's development as a soldier rather than as an artist.

In 1881 Bierce published the first of many Civil War writings, a personal memoir entitled "What I Saw of Shiloh." Toward the end of the piece Bierce makes a statement that serves as a fitting preface to all his war writing, both fiction and nonfiction, that would follow:

> In subordination to the design of this narrative, as defined by its title, the incidents related necessarily group themselves about my own personality as a center; and, as this center, during the few terrible hours of the engagement, maintained a variably constant relation to the open field already mentioned, it is important that the reader should bear in mind the topographical and tactical features of the local situation. (I: 257–58)[3]

Here Bierce himself outlines key features that mark his war stories. First is the emphasis on the verb *saw* and its stress, again, on personal witness. Consequently, he will attempt drawing his readers in because he and his experience will always be at the center of the work and will always make the reader, unwittingly or not, bear in mind the topographical and tactical features of the local situation. Therein also lies the primary justification for the organization and research methodology of this book. After all, if the Devil's Lexicographer himself claims, "it is important that the reader should bear in mind the topographical and tactical features of the local situation," then it only seems fitting to examine those features closely and carefully.

Chapter 1

Biography

Bierce's Military and Literary Worlds

> In all these exercises the book will be scrupulously
> followed.
> [...]
> The accompanying map was accurately drawn
> by my topographical officer on the spot, two or
> three days after the battle.
> Brigadier General William B. Hazen
> *A Narrative of Military Service* (1885)

In 1919, while Ernest Hemingway was recuperating from combat wounds
at his home in Oak Park, Illinois, he frequently walked to the library at the
nearby Scoville Institute. There, some British historians were compiling
detailed maps of the First World War. The maps allowed Hemingway to
see graphically the fighting he had witnessed and that his friend British
captain Edward Eric "Chink" Dorman-Smith had told him so much
about. Thirty years later, Hemingway recalled hiking with Dorman-Smith
in postwar Europe:

> Chink and I used to walk the great fights when we had leave after the
> first war and we would fight each other at any famous or infamous place
> like playing chess. We used to take and / or defend Pamplona till it was
> worse than [the U. S. Army's infantry training center at] Fort Benning
> (*Letters* 687).

Ambrose Bierce, whose stories Hemingway read, spent the last two years of the American Civil War as a military mapmaker. Twenty-two years after the end of the war, Bierce wrote in a newspaper column, "To this day I cannot look over a landscape without noting the advantages of the ground for attack or defense; here is an admirable site for an earthwork, there a noble place for a field battery" (qtd. in Fatout, *Lexicographer* 394). The point of Hemingway's comments is remarkably similar to Bierce's. Both these masters of the short story pride themselves on knowledge of the military aspects of terrain, and both enjoy war-gaming on terrain they visit. Unlike Hemingway, Bierce "was never the 'struggling' artist." He was a successful newspaper columnist whose war stories were "written late in life and simply as a divertissement" from his newspaper work (McWilliams 211). Before he was a newspaperman, Bierce was a soldier-topographer and, from all evidence, quite a good one.

The path that took Ambrose Gwinett Bierce into soldierhood was relatively direct. He was born on June 24, 1842, near Horse Cave Creek in Meigs County, Ohio. He was the youngest of ten surviving children of Marcus Aurelius and Laura Sherwood Bierce. Marcus A. Bierce was a voracious reader particularly fond of poetry, whose favorite works were those of Lord Byron. Unfortunately, the Bierce family was also extremely poor. Although characterized as "a dreamer and romanticist," the elder Bierce was a farmer and not an especially successful one (Fatout, *Lexicographer* 9). When Ambrose was four, the family moved to Kosciusko County, Indiana, in hopes of finding better farmland, and they settled on Goose Creek near the town of Warsaw. Here, Ambrose came of age under the Calvinistic upbringing of his parents and an unremarkable education in the local schools. Never able to get along with his parents, Ambrose left home at the age of fifteen and moved into Warsaw, where he worked for two years as a printer's devil for an abolitionist newspaper and boarded with the editor's family. This was his first exposure to the newspaper business.

In 1859, Bierce left Warsaw and went to live in Akron with his paternal uncle and "the family's resident great man," Lucius Verus Bierce (Morris 16). Greatly admired by young Ambrose, Lucius was a longtime member of a secret military society and became a general in the state militia. In 1838, he had helped to organize and lead an idealistic but ill-fated campaign against oppressive British government in Windsor, Canada. Uncle Lucius, a successful attorney and four-time mayor of Akron, was also an ardent supporter of John Brown and had gone so far as to help arm Brown and his followers from a disbanded militia store.

Thanks to the influence and deep pockets of his uncle, Ambrose Bierce enrolled at Kentucky Military Institute later in 1859. KMI was one of the South's most prestigious military high schools at the time, and, according to Morris, "featured a demanding curriculum of Latin composition, English grammar, and American history, along with supplemental courses in architecture, political science, physiology, mathematics, constitutional law, and physical education" (18). Unfortunately, a fire at the school destroyed many records and with them any documentary record of Bierce's time there. Although his time at the institute was relatively brief, most biographers believe it is where Bierce learned the rudiments of draftsmanship, military mapping, and topography. He spent only one school year at KMI and was back in Indiana the next summer.

In that summer of 1860, Bierce settled in Elkhart, about thirty miles north of Warsaw. On April 19, 1861, at the age of eighteen, he enlisted in Company C of the Ninth Regiment of Indiana Volunteers at Elkhart. Bierce was the second man in the county to enlist and was to remain in uniform for all but the final months of the Civil War. Bierce, who had been a rather unremarkable youth up to that time, was by all accounts, including wartime dispatches, an excellent soldier. He was to become a veteran of some of the war's bloodiest campaigns, including personal participation in three of the war's ten costliest battles: Shiloh, Stone's River, and Chickamauga.

Before turning to Bierce's war fiction, an overview of his service and his lifelong attraction to the military is helpful. One week after Bierce's enlistment, the entire regiment mustered in at Indianapolis. After a month of drill, the Ninth Regiment left by train for Grafton, West Virginia. The regiment spent the months of June and July in the Cheat Mountain country of West Virginia and participated in relatively minor engagements at Philippi, Laurel Hill, and Carrick's Ford. In these very early war days, Bierce's bravery first drew notice, and official reports cited him.

Because the Ninth had mustered in for a ninety-day term of service, it returned to Indianapolis in mid-July and was mustered out, reorganized, and returned to service in early September. Corporal Bierce was promoted to sergeant in August and then to sergeant major in September. The regiment returned to West Virginia and fought in battles at Greenbrier in October and Camp Allegheny in December. In February of 1862, the Ninth Regiment was assigned to General Don Carlos Buell's Army of the Ohio. The troops were immediately shipped to Nashville, where General Buell had just taken control. Once in Nashville, the regiment was assigned to General Nelson's Division of which

Colonel William B. Hazen's brigade was a part. The Ninth would remain a part of Hazen's Brigade for the remainder of the war.

The bloody fighting at Shiloh in April 1862 was the first test of the Ninth Regiment under Hazen, and the Indiana soldiers distinguished themselves on the second day of fighting. Hazen was promoted to brigadier general shortly afterward. The regiment spent the summer of 1862 in Kentucky and Tennessee, fighting in the battle at Perryville, Tennessee, in October. On the first of December, Ambrose Bierce was commissioned as a second lieutenant of infantry. Later that month, Hazen's Brigade played a critical role in the battle at Stone's River, Tennessee, just outside Murfreesboro. In March of 1863, Bierce was promoted to first lieutenant and moved to a position on the brigade staff as provost marshal. One month later, in April, he was appointed the brigade's acting topographic engineer, responsible for drawing maps for his unit. That same month, Hazen's Brigade became a part of General William S. Rosecrans's Army of the Cumberland.

The topographic engineer filled a vital staff position during the Civil War, and a more extended consideration of his duties is important. Detailed maps suitable for planning and executing military operations were sorely lacking for most parts of the country. The topographic engineer was the commander's personal mapmaker, who, along with the cavalry and other scouts, became his "eyes" prior to a battle. In "George Thurston," Bierce's first published piece of war fiction, the narrator is a topographic engineer who gives a revealing explanation of his duties:

> It was hazardous work; the nearer to the enemy's lines I could penetrate, the more valuable were my field notes and resulting maps. It was a business in which the lives of men counted as nothing against the chance of defining a road or sketching a bridge. Whole squadrons of cavalry escort had sometimes to be sent thundering against a powerful infantry outpost in order that the brief time between the charge and the inevitable retreat might be utilized in sounding a ford or determining the point of intersection of two roads. (II: 210)

The narrator of "George Thurston" goes on to explain that such expeditions "fixed in my memory a vivid and apparently imperishable picture of the locality—a picture [. . .]" (II: 210–11). Such pictures, made during his twenty-two months as a topographer, fill the war prose of Ambrose Bierce.

Paul Fatout comments on Bierce's technical skill in "Ambrose Bierce, Civil War Topographer," claiming that he "produced meticulous drawings: never an erasure, never a smudge. [. . .] The general craftsmanship is excellent" (396). Indeed, an early example of Bierce's work is a map he drew in November of 1863 of Brown's Ferry near Chattanooga (map

2). Especially impressive about the Brown's Ferry map are the detailed renderings of the complex contours of Raccoon Mountain and the ridge-line on the west bank of the Tennessee River. If one places a modern U.S. Geological Survey map, made with the assistance of aerial photography and computers, alongside Bierce's depiction of the same terrain (map 3),

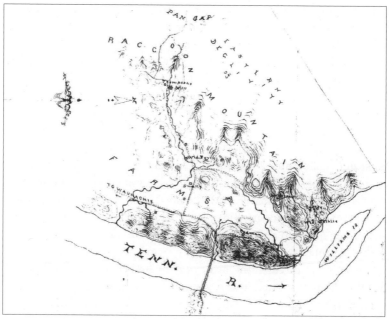

Map 2. Map of Brown's Ferry, Tennessee, drawn by Ambrose Bierce in November 1863. From Ambrose Bierce Collection (#5992), The Clifton Waller Barrett Library of American Literature, Special Collections, University of Virginia Library. Reprinted with permission.

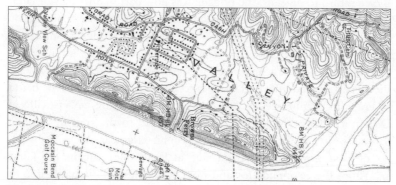

Map 3. Bierce's Brown's Ferry map alongside a current U.S. Geologic Survey map of the same terrain on the west side of the Tennessee River. The modern map was produced with the aid of satellite and aerial imagery as well as computer mapping techniques. The accuracy with which Bierce rendered the contours and relief of the same terrain testifies to his mapmaking skills.

one can begin to gain an appreciation for just how talented a field cartographer the young lieutenant was.

Bierce's duties as a mapmaker not only gave him an acute eye for the military aspects of terrain, they greatly expanded the scope of his personal vision of the war. Early in the war, as a private and then a sergeant, Bierce's experience was largely confined to the small-unit level. As a brigade staff officer, especially as a topographic engineer, Bierce was an important part of higher-level operational and tactical planning. He had daily contact with colonels and generals. His duties included coordination and relaying messages to higher and lower headquarters, and he had to travel over a much larger territory than would be possible as a foot soldier. This experience gave Bierce a comprehensive view of the war around him and provided him a unique and rich historical context he simply would not have had if he had spent the entire war as an infantryman.

The Army of the Cumberland spent the spring and summer of 1863 campaigning in central Tennessee. In September, Hazen's Brigade fought in the battle of Chickamauga, where Bierce was mentioned in dispatches for his distinguished service. In December, after the battles of Lookout Mountain and Missionary Ridge at Chattanooga, the Ninth Regiment was put on furlough for two months before returning to Hazen's Brigade for the Atlanta Campaign.

In February of 1864, the Army of the Cumberland became a part of Sherman's army, located in extreme northwestern Georgia. During the campaign for Atlanta, a Confederate sharpshooter wounded Bierce in the head at Kennesaw Mountain on June 23, 1864. After three months' convalescence in Indiana, Bierce returned to Atlanta and attempted to rejoin his brigade. Although Hazen had requested that Lieutenant Bierce return to his staff, the brigade was now part of Sherman's March to the Sea, and Bierce was assigned instead as a brigade topographic engineer in General Schofield's Fourth Army Corps. Schofield moved out of Atlanta at the end of September 1864 and dashed without resistance through northern Alabama into southern Tennessee by November. Bierce participated in two of the Confederacy's last offensives, the battle at Franklin, Tennessee, in November and the battle at Nashville in December. After Franklin, Bierce was moved to the staff of General Samuel Beatty as the division's topographic engineer. After Nashville, the division moved to winter quarters at Huntsville, Alabama. In January 1865, Bierce applied for and obtained a medical discharge due to complications from his head wound.

Bierce did not leave Alabama, but went immediately to work as a U.S. treasury agent charged with recovering abandoned and stolen federal property. Although not a part of his official duties, Bierce continued to draw maps and sketches of the terrain in southern Tennessee and northern Alabama even after the war.

In 1866, General Hazen was assigned to make an inspection of army posts in the Indian territory. Additionally, he was to survey and map the region. Hazen found his old topographic engineer and recruited him for the western expedition. Bierce stayed with Hazen until the team arrived in San Francisco six months later. After a failed attempt by Hazen to re-commission Bierce in the army as a captain, Bierce elected to remain in California.

Although the circumstances by which Bierce stayed in California were unfortunate, it was a place where he would ultimately flourish. While working in a low-level position at the U.S. Mint in San Francisco, Bierce began contributing essays and stories to local newspapers and became an editor in 1868. He contributed several sketches that appeared in the early 1870s to Bret Harte's *Overland Monthly*. Bierce married in late 1871, and his affluent father-in-law financed a three-year trip to England for the young couple. Bierce enjoyed his time overseas and immediately began contributing pieces to London newspapers and magazines. He experienced a moderate degree of success and published his first three books in England.

Upon returning to the United States in 1875, Bierce again took a minor position at the U.S. Mint in San Francisco and began to write a weekly column for a new local magazine called *The Argonaut*. In 1881, Bierce was hired as the editor of the weekly *San Francisco Wasp*, a position in which he flourished not only as editor but also as an opinionated, brutally satirical commentator on political, economic, and social affairs. Despite the *Wasp*'s success, the magazine's owner sold the publication and left Bierce without a job.

During his time at the *Wasp*, Bierce attracted the attention of William Randolph Hearst. In 1887, Hearst hired Bierce to write for the *San Francisco Examiner*. Finally Bierce had entered a period of professional success and economic stability. He continued to work for Hearst until the turn of the century. Bierce became the literary arbiter of the West Coast and his journalistic influence in political matters eventually caused his reputation to spread east as well. Hearst sent him on an extended assignment to Washington, DC, in 1896 to report on a railroad bill that would have caused millions of dollars of railroad debt to be forgiven at taxpayer expense. Bierce's scathing editorials in both the *New York Journal* and *San Francisco Examiner* were instrumental in ensuring the bill's defeat and further added to his reputation.

In 1899, Bierce relocated to Washington, DC, primarily to be near his second son. Despite his success, his life was marked by personal tragedies that included the death of his first son in a duel over a woman, long estrangement and eventual divorce from his wife, and the death from pneumonia of his second son just two years after Bierce moved to Washington. By 1901, at the age of sixty, Bierce began a sort of semi-retirement though he remained on the payroll and continued to contribute to Hearst magazines and newspapers for several more years.

Demonstrating the accuracy of Woodruff's assertion that "emotionally, he never left the army at all" (12), Bierce wrote the chief of staff of the army in late 1908 concerning "a theory and system of giving oral commands" (Papers). He was subsequently invited to the Army War College, which was, and still is, the Army's highest level training school for officers, to explain and demonstrate his theory. Just what impact the sixty-six-year-old former lieutenant had on the army cannot be determined; however, the president of the War College did send Bierce a follow-up letter thanking him and explaining, "The question is not whether your method of giving commands is good—all admit that—but of how to arrange for the giving of commands in that manner uniformly throughout the army; this is a matter which will require much thought" (Papers).

After three years of work editing his *Collected Works*, Bierce announced his intention to go to Mexico to report on the border incursions and rebellion of Pancho Villa. Although Bierce had bitterly criticized the Spanish-American War in Hearst's papers, he found the fighting in Mexico an irresistible attraction; like his 1908 appearance at the War College, it seemed to stir up his old military affinities. In 1912, Bierce wrote to one of his admirers, "This fighting in Mexico interests me. I want to go down there and see if those Mexicans can shoot straight." To another, he said, "I'm on my way to Mexico, because I like the game. I like the fighting; I want to see it. [. . .] I want to get at the true facts" (qtd. in Fatout 315). On his way to Mexico in October 1913, Bierce made an extensive tour of his old southern battlefields, visiting some of them for the third time since the Civil War. Sometime in late 1913 or early 1914, shortly after his arrival in Mexico, Bierce disappeared without a trace. The mystery has never been conclusively solved. Some think he was killed accidentally or after incurring the wrath of Villa's bandits. Others suspected he became an expatriate, living out his days in South America and writing under a pen name. Yet another theory claims that the Mexican reporting was a hoax, a cover story for a suicide with which Bierce intended to baffle the American public.

Ambrose Bierce's wartime association with William B. Hazen had a life-long impact. No person was more singularly responsible for Bierce's professional military development. If overstating the importance of military service of Bierce's life would be difficult, then overstating the importance of Hazen on Bierce's military service would be equally so. The two were, in fact, kindred spirits, both stubborn and extremely opinionated and each a sincere admirer of the other. Moreover, if elements of Bierce's war stories as essential as historical context, setting, and theme reflect his soldierly growth, then one could reasonably expect that Brigadier General Hazen's imprint would surface in them. William McCann characterizes Bierce's regard for Hazen most accurately and succinctly when he writes, "Only one soldier, William B. Hazen, seems to have come up to Bierce's notion of what a general should be" (v). Hazen, somewhat of a military misanthrope himself, has been characterized as "taciturn, grim and adamant. [. . .] His career was blotched by bad luck and the jealousy of rivals. [. . .] As a strategist and commander, he was probably the equal of Sherman or Thomas, but he was always falling into unfortunate quarrels. [. . .] His habit of bickering did not cease with the war" (McWilliams 48). A brief look at Hazen's career serves as an important foundation for an appreciation of Bierce's war fiction.

General Hazen, twelve years Bierce's senior, was a fellow midwesterner who had grown up in Ohio and graduated from West Point in 1855. In the following years, he distinguished himself as a battlefield commander, first on the western frontier fighting Indians, and then in the Civil War. After the war, Hazen gained a reputation as one of the best military minds in the country and pressed for extensive reforms in the army's organization and equipment.

For all his battlefield success, sternness, and reputation as a no-nonsense soldier, Hazen was no martinet. He had a surprising range of talents. In 1872, after President Grant sent Hazen on a lengthy observation trip to the Franco-Prussian War, Hazen published a book entitled *The School and the Army in Germany and France*, which called for significant tactical and logistical reforms to what he saw as a mismanaged, cumbersome United States Army. In 1875, Hazen published a pamphlet entitled "Some Corrections to My Life on the Plains," a rebuttal of General George Custer's *My Life on the Plains*. Back in 1868, while both were assigned to Indian duty, Hazen and Custer had disagreed about attacking bands that Hazen considered friendly. In at least one case, Hazen prevented Custer from attacking tribes that Hazen was confident were peaceful. Later in 1875, he published a short book entitled *Our Barren Lands* in which he presented his assessment of the potential of the High Plains for agricultural development. In it, Hazen was attempting to counter many propagandistic, overly optimistic predictions designed by speculators to attract settlers. Hazen, as Bierce would famously do during his time as a San Francisco reporter, took particular aim at the railroads, claiming, for example, "The Northern Pacific Railroad has taken up considerable space in these pages, because its partisans have continued to assert the value of these barren lands. But the truth, which can no longer be denied, is of far greater importance than the profit or loss from many railroads, serious as these interests may be" (*Narrative* 52). One must wonder if Bierce is here again imitating his mentor as he did in his years as a soldier.

The next year, Hazen was instrumental in causing the resignation of Secretary of War William W. Belknap for mismanagement of army-post traderships. Hazen had presented evidence that Belknap received sizeable personal kickbacks from civilian suppliers to western posts. In late 1880, President Rutherford B. Hayes appointed Hazen as chief signal officer of the army. The move was widely acclaimed in the press, and a comment in the *New York Tribune* on the day the appointment was confirmed reflects how well known and highly regarded the general was:

> Among the colonels in active service, it would be impossible to designate one better fitted by mental powers, scholarly habits and scientific tastes to fill the service. [. . .] [Hazen is] a representative of the element in the Army which studies hard and works hard, believes that an officer has something to do in time of peace besides drinking whiskey and playing cards, and does not think the old saying need ever be verified that a full colonelcy and complete imbecility come to a man at the same time. (qtd. in Baumgartner xxii).

In his capacity as chief signal officer, the former infantryman was instrumental in developing the fledgling Weather Bureau into a nationwide organization with established meteorological stations. Under his leadership, the Weather Bureau began to employ professional scientists as well as upgrade and rely more on instruments.

Hazen showed himself a talented soldier who was quite willing to take on what he saw as waste, fraud, and abuse by railroad and public officials in the 1870s and 1880s. These were exactly the sorts of things that Bierce made a name for himself by doing in print throughout the

1880s and 1890s, particularly with the defeat of the railroad bill in 1896. In a memoir called "The Crime at Pickett's Mill," Bierce characterizes Hazen as "a born fighter [. . .] the best hated man that I ever knew [. . .]. He was aggressive, arrogant, tyrannical, honorable, truthful, courageous— a skillful soldier" (I: 283, 284). Especially revealing about this description by "the most hated man in San Francisco" is that he would pen a string of adjectives about Hazen all of which had been used at various times to describe Bierce himself. Hazen's statement "I am always ready to cast stones at outrages" sounds so much like something Bierce the columnist would say that it succinctly highlights the thorough affinity the two shared (qtd. in Baumgartner v).

General Hazen provided both personal and professional support to Ambrose Bierce several times during Bierce's life. The career officer began doing so for the Indiana conscript not long after the latter began to work for him and continued throughout the war. In October 1863, after only six months as brigade topographic engineer, reorganization plans within the Army of the Cumberland would have removed the Ninth Indiana Volunteers from Hazen's Brigade. That meant any officers from the regiment that Hazen had placed on his own staff would leave and move with the regiment. Hazen personally requested that Bierce and one other officer, a surgeon, be permitted to remain on his staff. Army Headquarters approved the request. In August 1864, Hazen was given command of a division. In his final official report as brigade commander, the general gave special recognition to four of his battalion commanders and then wrote, "My staff has always rendered me most efficient service. Lieut. A. G. Bierce, my topographical officer, a fearless and trusty man, was severely wounded in the head before Kenesaw Mountain on the 23d of June" (*OR* 1/XXXVIII: 425).[1] The fact that Hazen cites Bierce immediately after four colonels who commanded battalions is another indication of Hazen's extremely high regard for the lieutenant. When Bierce returned to duty in September after convalescing from his wound, Hazen requested that Bierce again be assigned to his staff, claiming, "My reasons for asking this detail are that Lt. Bierce has served with me for a long time and I believe he will still be of great service to me, and greater service to the good in such capacity than any other" (Papers). This time, however, Hazen did not get his request, apparently because Bierce was still recuperating and had to be assigned to light duties that required no foot marching—something that would have been difficult to avoid entirely, even with a horse, in a division that was about to leave on Sherman's March to the Sea.

Probably the most widely known example of Hazen's postwar support of Bierce occurred during Hazen's 1866 inspection and mapping expedition. Bierce, who had been vacationing in Panama and New Orleans, immediately accepted the offer of civilian topographic attaché and joined Hazen in Omaha during the early summer. Waiting for Bierce in San Francisco was an offer of another army commission as a second lieutenant. But Hazen had requested a captaincy for his topographer, and both men were insulted by the offer. Roy Morris rightly points out, however, that given the armywide, postwar rank reductions (Hazen, who finished the war a major general, was now back down to colonel), "[i]t was a tribute to Bierce's war record that, as an unknown volunteer soldier from small-town Indiana, he had been offered any commission at all" (107). Bierce decided not to accept the commission. Years later he wrote that "ingratitude, more strong than traitors' arms, quite vanquished me: I resigned, parted from Hazen more in sorrow than in anger and remained in California" (I: 364). Hazen and Bierce corresponded with each other until Hazen's death in early 1887. Even as late as 1886, Hazen, then chief signal officer of the army, wrote a personal letter to the commissioner of pensions in an effort to correct a problem Bierce was having with his army pension (Papers). Here again, a year before his death, Hazen was helping his former protégé.

Clearly, William B. Hazen was a significant personal and professional influence on the character of Ambrose Bierce. If imitation is the highest form of flattery, then Hazen was one of very few (perhaps the only) men that Bierce unabashedly flattered. What also presents itself is the intriguing possibility that the man Bierce called "my commander and my friend, my master in the art of war" may have been a significant influence on Bierce's fiction as well. Certainly up until the time of Hazen's death, the general was outpublishing the newspaperman as far as books were concerned. His final effort was a memoir, largely of the Civil War, entitled *A Narrative of Military Service*.[2] In December 1885, Hazen remarked in a short letter to Bierce, "My new book, 'A Narrative of Military Service,' will soon be out" (Papers). In the book, Hazen characterizes his former topographic engineer as "a brave and gallant fellow [. . .] now well known in California for rare literary abilities" (265n) and includes two, or possibly three, of Bierce's wartime maps as illustrations.

In 1929, scholar Napier Wilt noted connections between Bierce's own memoirs and Hazen's. Exactly when Bierce read Hazen's book cannot be determined, but in May 1888 the *San Francisco Examiner* published a short Bierce memoir entitled "The Crime at Pickett's Mill" that confirms Bierce had indeed read it by then. Bierce quotes directly from several official reports of the battle that appear in Hazen's chapter on Pickett's Mill. Near the end of "The Crime at Pickett's Mill," Bierce begins a sentence with "Hazen in his 'Narrative of Military Service' says [. . .]" (I: 295). What is especially significant about the timing here is that only one Bierce memoir, "What I Saw of Shiloh," and two war stories, "George Thurston" along with the satire "Jupiter Doke," predate publication of Hazen's memoir. The years 1888 through 1891, immediately after publication of Hazen's memoir and his death, were Bierce's most prolific and were when he wrote all his war stories with the exception of a few wartime ghost tales. The publication history not only of memoirs, but of Bierce's war fiction as well, strongly suggests that General Hazen's book was a major influence. Most of Bierce's stories first appeared between 1887 and 1891 in the San Francisco *Wasp*, a weekly Bierce edited, and Hearst's *Examiner*, for which he was a columnist. In other words, it is significant that the fiction Bierce is most remembered for began to appear in quantity starting just over a year after Hazen published his book and only months after his death. It seems reasonable that Bierce could have been inspired by Hazen's memoir as well as by the sight of some of his own maps among its pages. This further strengthens the point that Bierce's war stories are primarily a reflection of his own journey through the war. The war, Bierce's role in it, Hazen's mentorship, and his later influence on the production of Bierce's retellings in both memoir and fiction are intricately intertwined.

Chapter 2

Early War Stories

1861, West Virginia

> I see omens of chaos, Krishna; I see no good in killing my kinsmen in battle.
> [. . .]
> Krishna, we have heard that a place in hell is reserved for men who undermine family duties.
>> Bhagavad Gita

> CHRISTIAN, *n.* One who follows the teachings of Christ in so far as they are not inconsistent with a life of sin.
> PILGRIM, *n.* A traveler that is taken seriously.
>> *The Devil's Dictionary*

For Ambrose Bierce and his fellow soldiers in the Ninth Indiana Infantry, the early days of the Civil War must have seemed a grand adventure indeed. The vast majority of the Ninth was from northwest and north central Indiana, an area remarkable, with the exception of the Lake Michigan shore, for its lack of distinctive terrain features. From this area, where most of the population were farmers and the most important cash crops were wheat and corn, the men of the Ninth Regiment were sent to the mountain country along the eastern side of what is now West Virginia. The difference in terrain is truly remarkable. Bierce wrote of it: "To a member of a plains-born tribe, born and reared on the flats of

Ohio or Indiana, a mountain region is a perpetual miracle. Space seemed to have taken on a new dimension" (I, 227). Northwestern Indiana is about eight hundred feet above sea level, and the elevation may change less than sixty feet over a number of miles. Eastern West Virginia has mountains that typically exceed four thousand feet and elevation changes in excess of two thousand feet within two miles. Added to this was the fact that for the summer and early fall of 1861 the fighting that the Ninth did in West Virginia amounted, as Bierce claimed in retrospect, to little more than skirmishing.

In 1864, a year before the war's end, an omnibus volume of partial regimental histories entitled *Indiana's Roll of Honor* was published and contained the following revealing passage:

> It is singular how wandering through the mountains became a passion with the men. For days and nights, and sometimes for a week, they would lie out in the deep solitudes which intervened between the opposing forces, watching for some sign of life in the enemy's camp, or tracking his scouts to intercept or circumvent them. An intimation that a few men were wanted to go in front, would at any time crowd the headquarters with applicants. They had all been on an outpost picket in turn, and became infatuated with the idea of scaling the rugged peaks which lifted their head on every side, and of exploring the deep intervening valleys and ravines, where the silence of the grave seemed to reign. The regular scouts were regarded with a species of reverence. As they related their adventures around the camp-fires at night, the young soldiers sighed to emulate their exploits, and looked anxiously forward to the time when they could tell how they had groped their way alone through the laurel thickets. Many of the scouts scaled the summits of moss-covered rocks, slept for nights behind a log, watching the clear stars shining above them [. . .] and after days and nights of privation, deemed themselves sufficiently rewarded by the sight of an enemy's camp on a distant hillside. (Stevenson 159–60)

What is remarkable about this passage is the consistency of its tone and, to some degree, its language with Bierce's own memoirs of and correspondence about West Virginia. When he published the memoir "On a Mountain" as a selection in Volume I of *The Collected Works*, Bierce wrote of the region:

> Looking back upon it through the haze of near half a century, I see that region as a veritable realm of enchantment; the Alleghenies as the Delectable Mountains. I note again their dim, blue billows, ridge after ridge interminable, beyond purple valleys full of sleep, 'in which it seemed

always afternoon.' Miles and miles away, where the lift of earth meets the stoop of sky, I discern an imperfection in the tint, a faint graying of the blue above the main range—the smoke of an enemy's camp. (I: 225)

Further remembering, Bierce claims that West Virginia "was an enchanted land. How we reveled in its savage beauties! With what pure delight we inhaled its fragrances of spruce and pine! How we stared with something like awe at its clumps of laurel! [. . .] We ascended every hill within our picket-lines and called it a 'peak.'" (I: 227–28) Here Bierce's own words echo the experiences described in the 1864 history. His use of the term "Delectable Mountains" is a fairly obvious allusion to John Bunyan's *The Pilgrim's Progress.* It is a resonance in language and imagery that surfaces in his war fiction of the period as well.

Bierce wrote two memoirs of his wartime service in West Virginia: "A Bivouac of the Dead," first published after he revisited the area in 1903, and "On a Mountain," first published in 1909 in volume I of *The Collected Works of Ambrose Bierce.* These two deeply retrospective pieces serve as frames for much of *The Collected Works.* Bierce published "On a Mountain" as the lead piece in a section of volume I entitled "Bits of Autobiography." "A Bivouac of the Dead" reappeared as the final piece in volume XI, *Antepenultima.*[1] What is significant about the positioning of the West Virginia memoirs is their appearance in places of apparent privilege within the overall structure of the twelve-volume *Collected Works.* In "A Bivouac of the Dead," Bierce compares the rude Confederate graves in a farm field to the well-tended, immaculate Federal cemetery at Grafton.[2] For this final bit of autobiography in his penultimate book, it is as if he is coming full circle back to West Virginia where his combat service began. It is a circle that he makes in his fiction as well.

Even in these "halcyon days" as he referred to them in a memoir, Ambrose Bierce was beginning to distinguish himself as a soldier. A history of Indiana's participation in the war published in 1866 tells of fighting near Laurel Hill in early July 1861:

> In the attack, two soldiers, Bierce and Boothroyd, advanced within fifteen paces of the enemy's fortifications, and here Boothroyd received a wound in the neck, which paralyzed him. His comrade immediately caught him in his arms and carried him and his gun full twenty rods, bullets falling around them at every step. (Merrill 49)

Here, only one month after arriving in West Virginia, Bierce was beginning to render the "efficient service" that would mark his time in the army and lay the foundation for his relatively rapid rise through the ranks.

What emerges from these memoirs and histories is a sense of just how strongly one might expect Bierce's own experience in West Virginia to inform the themes and setting of war stories he locates there. It should come as no surprise that the settings of these stories are typically vague, often simply dense forests, and the stories involve a lone soldier on some type of sentry duty. This is how Bierce spent much of his time while he was in West Virginia, especially during the initial three months service in the summer of 1861. Bierce was a private then and had a private's view of the war. He doubtless spent significant amounts of time standing a watch alone on guard duty through the night, confronting personal fears as well as the enemy, and reacting to situations in which established personal ethics and loyalties seemed at odds with military duty.

Indeed within the events of these stories Bierce stays largely within the limits of his own experience. The world of the West Virginia stories is not a world of generals and grand strategy, of incompetent high-level decisions that will send many soldiers to their deaths. Instead, one finds a world of the individual soldier faced with personal dilemmas, knowing little else about the war than the ground he is standing on and what he sees around him. This is substantially the same world as that of Henry Fleming in *The Red Badge of Courage*. And, while the land was indeed enchanting, it also contained the element of death. Beguiling as the forests and peaks were by day, there is no doubt that to the young "flat-landers who invaded the Cheat Mountain country" it could be terrifying when one was alone at night on sentry duty (I: 227). Further, as a private and then a young sergeant, Bierce would have had little access to maps or any sort of higher level plans. As a result, his memories of these places would be primarily what the eye could see.

Because they have such a dramatic impact on a combat soldier's daily existence, it is not unusual for him to remember landscapes and individual terrain features vividly yet have no idea of where those features fit in the larger context of regional geography. Indeed, in many cases a foot soldier has no idea exactly where he is or knows it only as a place-name heard from others. Lacking maps with which to place the terrain, and consequently the memory of it, into a larger context, it is no surprise that when he wrote the West Virginia stories, Bierce was doing so from his memories as a private and young sergeant. Hence the settings and terrain are vague and general—not unlike the B-movie cliché "somewhere in France, Autumn, 1944." Chances are that much of the time Private Bierce did not know exactly where he was when he was there.

"A Tough Tussle" is an appropriate story to begin examining Bierce's war fiction. Although it was the sixth war story he published, the date of the action of the story is the earliest. It is also his first story that takes place in, as the narrator describes it, the "region [that] was one of the wildest on the continent—the Cheat Mountain country" (III: 106). First published in the *San Francisco Examiner* in September 1888, the story tells of Second Lieutenant Brainerd Byring, a young Federal who is a "brave and efficient officer" but is beset with an aversion to the sight of dead bodies, an aversion that becomes an all-consuming phobia.[3] While on guard by himself in a quiet, wooded spot, he discovers the corpse of a Confederate nearby. As night sets in, the presence of the corpse becomes increasingly unnerving. Byring begins to think himself a coward; he even considers abandoning his post, but "he feared they would think he feared the corpse. He was no coward and he was unwilling to incur anybody's ridicule" (III: 115). But Byring is terrified of the corpse and begins to rationalize his fear as some atavistic trait from pagan ancestors. Later in the night there is a brief skirmish near Byring's position. Early the next morning, a surgeon and a small party of stretcher bearers search the area for the dead and wounded. They find Byring run through with his own sword and the corpse, obviously dead several days, "frightfully gashed and stabbed" with fresh wounds (III: 120).

"A Tough Tussle" demonstrates a motif that was to be one of Bierce's primal scenes, namely the lone soldier who must confront the extraordinary machinations of his own psyche. Frequently Bierce overlays one of his most common themes, the nature of courage and cowardice, on such a scene. Certainly the setting of the story is primal: the narrator describes it by saying, "The forest was boundless" and "The universe was one primeval mystery of darkness, without form and void" (III: 111), a description that echoes the primeval scene of Genesis 1.2: "And the earth was without form, and void; and darkness was upon the deep." Byring seems, in his own mind, to be "the sole, dumb questioner of its eternal secret" (III: 111). It is in such a setting that the lieutenant must confront his most basic fear, namely of "thinking a dead body a malign thing endowed with some strange power of mischief," a feeling that Byring rationalizes must have come from "our barbarous ancestors" on "the plains of Central Asia" (III: 113).

Details provided about the terrain are significant in another important respect. It is very indistinguishable and could be most anywhere in the Cheat Mountain country. Bierce provides nothing remarkable or identifiable about the terrain features of the setting, only that it is night near "the fork of an old wood-road" in a "boundless" forest (III: 107, 111). Except for the very end, the story occurs in moonlight. Here, as in almost all of the West Virginia stories, the setting is vague, obscured, and has the quality of something dimly remembered rather than a sharply focused, detailed description. This seems somewhat unusual for a writer who, according to Daniel Aaron's earlier observation, "managed to fix in his mind the terrain he had traversed and to map his stories and sketches so that the reader can visualize every copse or ravine or stream he mentions" ("Ambrose Bierce" 172). This paucity of detail is, however, entirely in keeping with Bierce's experience as an individual infantryman during the West Virginia campaign.

Bizarre as the story is, it has some remarkably autobiographic touches and demonstrates Bierce's penchant for writing about places and events as they were while he was there. Byring is a "brave and efficient officer" (III: 108), a description certainly evocative of William B. Hazen's postwar description of Bierce as "a brave and gallant fellow" (*Narrative* 265n). Byring enlisted "in the very first days of the war," as did Bierce. Byring "had been make first-sergeant of his company on account of his education and engaging manner" (III: 108). Bierce was made first-sergeant of his company, though his manner, as his hometown paper noted at the news, was not engaging, and one must wonder if this is a bit of sarcasm or self-parody. More than likely, incidents such as the rescue of Private Boothroyd, not personal charm, were more significant in Bierce's rapid rise through the enlisted ranks. Byring, like Bierce, also received a battlefield commission, though Bierce's came much later in the war. For Byring to be a lieutenant by the fall of 1861 is indeed an achievement. Byring has also been in the engagements at Philippi, Rich Mountain, Carrick's Ford, and Greenbrier—all places where Bierce and the Ninth Indiana Infantry fought prior to the Cheat Mountain campaign (map 4). Finally, though perhaps least significant, is the fact that the author's initials are *AB* and his protagonist's are *BB*. Normally, such a detail could certainly be dismissed as coincidence; however, in view of the number of clear autobiographical connections, it gives one pause.

Thematically, "A Tough Tussle" demonstrates an elemental and near-universal concern on a first-time combatant's mind: his reaction to the sight of suffering and death. Such questions as "How will I react to the possibility of my own maiming and death?" and "How will I react to the presence of death around me?" are essentially variations on what military historian John Keegan has identified as "the central question" of a soldier, "'How would *I* behave in a battle?'" (18). That such concerns were on Bierce's mind early in the war is borne out not only by the protagonists of his West Virginia stories, but by the memoir "On a Mountain" as well. In it, the author illustrates the irresistibility of confronting mor-

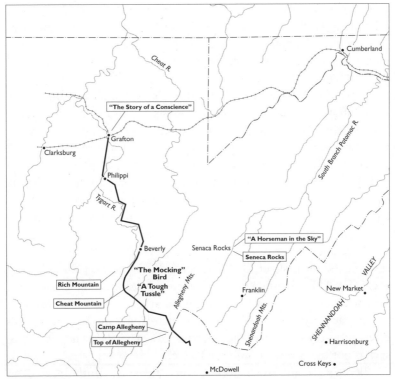

Map 4. Bierce in West Virginia. The heavy line shows the general route of the Ninth Indiana Volunteers in the West Virginia campaigns. The small flags pinpoint the locations of stories and related points of interest.

bidity when he and a few comrades spot "some things" during a halt in a march that turn out to be covered corpses:

> we examined them, curiously lifting the blankets from their yellow-clay faces. How repulsive they looked with their blood smears, their blank, staring eyes, their teeth uncovered by contraction of the lips! [. . .] We were as patriotic as ever, but we did not wish to be that way. (I: 232–33)

Fortunately, the regiment moved on and Bierce did not have to spend the night with the bodies, but he does note, "For an hour afterward the injunction of silence in the ranks was needless."

Even the allusion to the book of Genesis that appears in "A Tough Tussle" is relevant to the point. The story is a genesis in several senses of the word. First, because chronologically by time of plot it is the earliest of Bierce's Civil War stories, it is the genesis of his retelling of the war. Next, it is a story set in a time and place that represents Bierce's genesis as a combat soldier. The fundamental issues that Byring must deal with are among the most very basic in a new soldier's mind. Finally, then, it is the genesis of the notion that Bierce's professional development as a soldier, rather than his artistic development as a writer, is the more significant influence on his war fiction.

Although "A Tough Tussle" was Bierce's sixth published war story, it demonstrates a faulty level of craftsmanship that is not consistent with his best work. A prominent example occurs when a first-person narrator suddenly breaks into the tale for three sentences. The first, "I repeat that Lieutenant Byring was a brave and intelligent man," is jarring enough (III: 117). To make matters worse, the narrator then asks two questions directly of the reader rather than limiting himself in free indirect speech to asking questions, as the hitherto third-person narrative voice had, that only Byring could silently ask himself. Additionally, in an apostrophic–sounding aside to the reader, the narrator exclaims, "Ah, children of the sunlight and the gaslight, how little you know of the world in which you live!" (III: 111). Artistic shortcomings such as these are indicative of the somewhat uneven quality of Bierce's war stories. One might expect a reasonably steady trend of improving or declining quality as a writer's career progresses, but with the exception of a general decline at the end, such is not the case with Ambrose Bierce.

Bierce's second West Virginia story, the much-anthologized "A Horseman in the Sky," first appeared in the *San Francisco Examiner* in April 1889, seven months after "A Tough Tussle." The story was to reappear as the lead story in *Tales of Soldiers and Civilians* with good reason—it is among his best and certainly hardest hitting. "A Horseman in the Sky" tells of Carter Druse, a young West Virginian who enlists in a Federal regiment early in the war. His enlistment is much against the wishes of his staunchly Confederate and taciturn father, who characterizes his son as a traitor to Virginia. Months later, Druse is on sentry duty not far from his home on a sunny autumn afternoon in 1861. He watches from the top of a thousand-foot cliff that overlooks a valley where five regiments of Federal infantry are encamped for the day before attempting a night infiltration. Any disclosure of the Federals' position will compromise the element of surprise and hence the entire operation. The encampment is also in a valley that is hemmed in on all sides, a "military rat-trap" according to the narrator (II: 17). The dozing sentinel suddenly awakens to the sight of a Confederate scout on horseback who is also along the top of the cliff. Druse must decide what to do. There is no chance to capture the scout, and if he rides away, the five Federal regiments could be trapped in the valley by a small Confederate force. Even the possibility that the scout has seen nothing of the regiments in the valley evaporates when Druse looks down and sees troops foolishly watering their horses "in plain view of a dozen summits" (II: 22). Druse prepares himself to take his shot, the scout appears to look directly at him, and he steels himself remembering his father's last words to him, "Whatever may occur, do what you conceive to be your duty" (II: 23). Finally, Druse fires, but at the last second he drops his aim to the horse rather than the rider. The horse and rider pitch forward over the edge of the cliff and, with the rider keeping his seat the entire distance, plummet to the forest one thousand feet below. The sergeant of the guard makes his way to Druse's position a few minutes later and asks for a report. Druse reports he shot a horse that fell over the cliff. When asked if anyone was on the horse, Druse replies, "My father" (II: 26).

"A Horseman in the Sky" is Bierce's most memorable use of the lone sentry motif. Unlike Lieutenant Byring, the struggle Druse must confront is more an extraordinary moral dilemma than a psychological one. Druse faces one of the most difficult situations imaginable—the story has even been used as discussion material in military ethics classes at West Point.

Unlike Carter Druse, Bierce never had to confront a kinsman on the wrong end of a gun during the Civil War. The only other member of his family who fought was his older brother Albert, an artilleryman in an Ohio battery. Ambrose and Albert's only known encounter during the war was an amiable one when the two met by happenstance and chatted during the thick of the fighting at Chickamauga, Georgia. However, the story does have other connections with Bierce's West Virginia experiences. The tactical situation described in "A Horseman in the Sky" corresponds very roughly with the type of maneuver Union forces attempted against the Confederates at Camp Allegheny, West Virginia, in December 1861. As Bierce recounts in his memoir, "On A Mountain," the movement

> was to be made on the enemy's position miles away, at the summit of the main ridge of the Alleghanies—the camp whose faint blue smoke we had watched for weary days. The movement was made [. . .] over unknown roads by untrusty guides, encountering obstacles not foreseen [. . .] to execute the movement with requisite secrecy and precision.
>
> All one bright wintry day we marched down from our eyrie; all one bright wintry night we climbed the great wooded ridge opposite. (I: 231–32)

In "Horseman," the narrator explains that the regiments of Federal infantry

> had marched all the previous day and night [. . .]. At nightfall they would take to the road again, climb to the place where their unfaithful sentinel now slept, and descending the other slope of the ridge fall upon a camp of the enemy [. . .]. Their hope was to surprise it [. . .]. (II: 17)

Although the timing is certainly a bit off, that is, "Horseman" occurs on a "sunny afternoon in the autumn of the year 1861" and the fight at Camp Allegheny "one bright wintry day" (Friday, December 13, 1861, to be precise), the scenario in the short story, as in almost all of Bierce's war fiction, is faithful to the historical context.

Other, lesser events may have helped inspire "A Horseman in the Sky." Like most any mountain country, the West Virginia mountains are rich in local lore. Several regional tales have affinities with "A Horseman in the Sky." The War Department's official records of H Company of the Twenty-fourth Ohio Regiment record the death of a soldier "who was killed by falling over a precipice" while on the march in October 1861, precisely the time of the story (*Supplement* 677). A more apocryphal local story, perhaps an embellishment of the official one just mentioned, is of a Union soldier who fell off a cliff and met a grisly death when he landed in a den of rattlesnakes. Most important, however, is a local legend concerning one William Sites, who lived in a homestead across the road from the thousand-foot Tuscarora Cliffs and fought for the Confederacy. Oral tradition claims that a Union sniper killed Sites from a vantage point atop the cliffs in 1862. Falling off and shooting from the cliffs in the Cheat Mountain country appear to have been attractive motifs for the local storytellers. Doubtless Bierce and every other soldier in the Ninth Indiana heard of their comrade from a sister regiment, the Twenty-fourth Ohio, who fell to his death. The rattlesnake version seems an obvious embellishment as the story circulated through the Union camps.[4]

The most important geographic feature in the story, the thousand-foot cliff, is a remarkable piece of terrain. Cliffs of this size are relatively rare—many readers probably fail to grasp just how high that is. The observation deck at Chicago's Sears Tower, for example, is on the ninety-fourth floor and is one thousand feet above ground level. Were Bierce not a topographer who knew exactly what a thousand-foot cliff would look like, it would be easy to dismiss the claim that "a stone dropped from its edge would have fallen sheer downward one thousand feet to the tops of the pines" as simply a bit of authorial hyperbole (II: 16). But to pinpoint an actual location for this story is not difficult. A cliff of such remarkable height in West Virginia should be easy to find, especially given that Druse's home is "but a few miles from where he now lay" in the story, and that home is near the town of Grafton (II: 18). Roughly thirty miles northeast of Cheat Mountain, thirty miles from Camp Allegheny, and fifty miles from Grafton is Seneca Rocks, where the sandstone Tuscarora Cliffs loom one thousand feet high over the floor of the South Branch Valley.

In "A Horseman in the Sky" there is "a line of giant cliffs similar to those upon" which Druse and his father perch (II: 16). At Seneca Rocks there is indeed a line of similar cliffs (though not as high) running southwest from Tuscarora Cliffs. As is the case in several other Bierce stories, however, the terrain is not a perfect match. The road along which Carter Druse sleeps ascends southward, turns west along the summit, and then turns south again before winding down into the valley. That road does not exist, nor did it ever. There are trails that go up Tuscarora Cliffs, but the roads in and out of the valley, unsurprisingly, avoid the cliffs themselves.

Given the evidence, one can confidently claim that the Seneca Rocks inspired the setting of "A Horseman in the Sky." Bierce was in the area throughout the fall and winter of 1861, it is not far from Grafton, and the tactical situation that the narrator describes is a rough fit with a battle that occurred approximately thirty miles from the rocks. There is even a local legend about a Union sniper shooting from the cliffs, and though Bierce was an enlisted soldier and not a topographer at the time, Tuscarora Cliffs impress most anyone who sees them, particularly someone from the flatlands around Elkhart, Indiana.

However, Bierce stops short of naming the place specifically or of being absolutely accurate in his description. Here he establishes another pattern that will reemerge in many of his tales. An actual terrain feature, either natural or man-made, figures prominently in the story. Bierce does not, however, identify the feature by name and changes or obscures specifics just enough so that placing the location is possible only after some fairly detailed research. In other stories, however, Bierce will call the setting by its actual name and provide very specific details. What begins to emerge is a general pattern of craft choices that the author makes. In a story such as "Horseman," which involves a protagonist under extraordinary psychological or moral duress (or both), Bierce tends to modify existing features into a composite setting appropriate for the action, consequently the observation that these topographic twists are never wholly fictional, nor are they entirely factual. Certainly an obvious question is why alter the terrain—why not simply use it as it is? The more apparent point is that the terrain itself might not do exactly what Bierce needs it to do. To identify a piece of actual terrain and then make alterations for a story is to risk authorial credibility—to have a reader familiar with the countryside recognize obvious artistic liberties and thus question the quality of verisimilitude so central to the successful war story. More important, to locate an event as extraordinary as the central one in "A Horseman in the Sky" on an actual landmark is to risk believability in yet another way. It is to have the reader who is familiar with the territory know that such an event never occurred there. Hence the reader's reaction goes from "I wonder if that really happened?" to "I know that never happened there."

Irony is certainly another feature in this story. There is, as Mary Grenander has pointed out, the irony of the fact that the sleeping Druse would have been punished with death had he been discovered asleep at his post. Instead, he is, in a sense, punished by having to kill his father. There is irony in the fact that Druse's father's final words to his son—"Whatever may occur, do what you conceive to be you duty"—are the very words that cause Druse to make the decision to kill his father (II: 23). There is a minor bit of irony in the fact that the Federal officer on the ground who witnesses the fantastic plunge of horse and rider feels that he cannot tell his commander the truth about what he has seen because the truth seems so unbelievable and "he knew better than to tell an incredible truth" (II: 25). Yet the most significant irony, indeed the one that the story turns on, has been strangely overlooked by critics, perhaps because the climactic thousand-foot plunge at the end of the story has such an impact on most all who read it.

The penultimate sentence of the second section of the story, in which "the spirit had said to the body: 'Peace, be still,'" is extraordinarily significant (II: 23). Many readers may recognize in the quotation the words of Christ when he calmed the sea (Mark 4.39). Jesus and several disciples are in a boat when a storm suddenly rolls in. The disciples are frightened, but Jesus, who has been asleep in the back of the boat, awakens, speaks the words "Peace, be still," (even Bierce's punctuation is identical to the King James Version) and immediately, "the wind ceased and there was a great calm." Druse is also described as "calm" just prior to firing the fatal shot (II: 23). The parallel is further strengthened by the fact that both Druse and Christ were asleep at the beginning of the stories. In both, witnesses to the incidents have similar reactions. In the biblical story, the disciples in the boat are terrified "and they feared exceedingly" after Jesus speaks (Mark 4.41). In the Bierce tale, the officer at the bottom of the cliff is "[f]illed with amazement and terror by this apparition of a horseman in the sky" and he feels himself "the chosen scribe of some new Apocalypse" (II: 24), precisely the role of John in the Revelation. These biblical parallels point to the central irony of Bierce's tale—namely a reversal of the New Testament story. In "Horseman," "the spirit had said to the body: 'Peace, be still'"; in the Gospel of Mark, the body, or Christ incarnate, says to the wind, "Peace, be still." However, the greatest reversal of the New Testament is a more fundamental one. The synoptic gospels tell the story of God the Father sacrificing his Son to save many, while Bierce tells the story of a son who must sacrifice his godlike father— the narrator even describes him as like "a Grecian god carved in the marble"—to save the many souls camped in the "military rat-trap," the potential valley of death, below (II: 19). In a final bit of biblical reversal, the fundamental action of Bierce's tale is of the father descending and thus taking permanent leave of the son through death, while the biblical action is of the Son ascending for an eternal unification and life with the Father.

Unlike Carter Druse, Private William Grayrock, the protagonist of "The Mocking-Bird" does not sleep on duty. He is, however, like others in the West Virginia stories, alone. As in "A Tough Tussle," the setting is "a forest's heart in the mountain region of southwestern Virginia" (II: 218). (Here one must remember that during the war, West Virginia was still called western Virginia.) There are no distinct or identifying features; the location is vague, primal, and, as night falls, increasingly surreal and ominous. The previous night the twenty-four-year-old Grayrock had been on picket duty on the same spot and had fired at someone who had approached his post without responding to Grayrock's order to halt. Grayrock's shot set off a volley from other nervous sentinels who then retreated back to the Union lines. Grayrock alone remained at his post. The next day, a Sunday, he is given an afternoon pass for his bravery. Feeling unsettled because he knows his shot hit someone, he returns to his post of the previous night. He leans against a tree in the warm afternoon, dozes, and begins dreaming of his twin brother, from whom he was separated after their widowed mother's death. Following an idyllic childhood, each had gone to live with relatives, William in the North, John in the South. Around sunset, a mockingbird's call awakens William. The bird's song reminds him of a mockingbird that their mother had kept and that had figured prominently in his dream of youth. William follows the bird and in the fading sunset discovers whom he had shot in the darkness. It is, of course, his brother John, whose body is still warm. That night, when roll is called at the Federal camp, Grayrock is not there to answer, and is never seen again.

A significant portion of "The Mocking-Bird" does not take place in the actual landscape of West Virginia, but in the landscape of Private William Grayrock's afternoon dream. His dream vision, in fact, evokes loose but nevertheless clear parallels with Bunyan's *The Pilgrim's Progress*. Grayrock's dream vision begins with the words "[a]nd sleeping he dreamed" (II: 225); Christian's in *The Pilgrim's Progress* begins with "[a]nd as I slept I dreamed a Dream" (142). As Bierce does in the memoir "On a Mountain," the narrator then lapses into a Bunyanesque sequence of place-names. William and John, for example, live in an idyllic place between the Realm of Conjecture and the Enchanted Land, which lies beyond the great river. Interestingly enough, the brother who goes to the Enchanted Land has, like Bunyan, John as his given name. Like Christian, William is a naïve protagonist who makes a journey that is a quest for enlightenment. The fact that William's quest takes place in the Civil War world of Ambrose Bierce dooms it to end in an inevitably tragic enlightenment. This is, of course, the case when William discovers that the man he shot is his twin brother, John.

The central image of the story is not a terrain or geographic feature; it is the mockingbird of the title. The bird becomes an emblem of John himself. It is John who, once the brothers are separated as boys, keeps the caged mockingbird that had been at the door of the Grayrock's boyhood home. In words that both foreshadow the last ones in the story and that echo Chief Joseph's famous surrender message, William is to hear the song of a mockingbird "no more forever," that is, until it leads him to John's "still warm" body (II: 227, 229). John's body with "its gray uniform stained with a single spot of blood upon the breast, its white face turned sharply upward" replicates the colors of the bird's plumage, even in the fact that the bird's normally gray and white feathers are "flushed with sunset's crimson glory" (II: 228, 229). Upon William's discovery, the bird "stilled her song" (II: 229).

At the conclusion of the story the narrator tells the reader, "At roll-call that evening in the Federal camp the name William Grayrock brought no response, nor ever again thereafter" (II: 229). Most critics commenting on the story assume, as does Roy Morris, that William never answers again because, faced with the awful consequences of his shot in the dark, he has killed himself. Such a reading is certainly plausible, especially given the suicidal fate of Biercean protagonists in "A Tough Tussle," "One Officer, One Man," and "The Story of a Conscience." But the centrality of the mockingbird imagery suggests another possibility. Following William's discovery of the body, the bird falls silent and it "glided silently away through the solemn spaces of the wood" (II: 229). It is equally plausible that William, now becoming the inheritor of the bird's legacy, simply does likewise and deserts the army, perhaps returning through the terrain of his dream to the Enchanted Land of his brother. Desertion was an all too common problem during the Civil War, especially in many volunteer units.

Bierce published "The Mocking-Bird" almost two years after "A Horseman in the Sky." By that time he had published some of his best war stories, notably, "An Occurrence at Owl Creek Bridge." Yet, here again, as in "A Tough Tussle," there are craft shortcomings that detract from the story, the principal one being an abrupt intrusion by a seemingly omniscient first-person narrator. The narrator's comment is on tactical security lessons learned later in the war at Shiloh—an event that would not happen until April of 1862, roughly seven months after the action described in "The Mocking-Bird." The narrator then apologizes for his interruption claiming, "This is perhaps a vain digression. I should not care to undertake to interest the reader in the fate of an army; what we have here to consider is that of Private Grayrock" (II: 219). As much of an interruption as this is in the short story, it is entirely in keeping with Bierce's character. He no doubt found it irresistible to interject comment, via a nameless narrative voice, on practices that he now recognized as naïve and foolish in the early days of the war. After all, Bierce had been making a living as a newspaper columnist for several years by highlighting similar lapses in government, business, and organized religion in and around San Francisco. Fortunately, however, he stifled any such editorial urges when writing "A Horseman in the Sky."

In no other group of Bierce's stories does religious imagery figure quite so prominently as in his West Virginia stories. Why all three of the West Virginia stories draw heavily on allusions to either the Bible or *The Pilgrim's Progress* has an autobiographical connection as well, a connection that reflects the very earliest stages of his development as a soldier. More specifically, it is a reflection of a person making the transition from civilian to soldier. When he was a young soldier in West Virginia, the previous experiences of his life, with the exception of the year at Kentucky Military Institute, had been largely limited to the family farm and environs of Elkhart. Simply put, biblical literature was the reading Bierce knew best when he came into the Union army. He once explained, "My father was a poor farmer and could give me no general education, but he had a good library, and to his books I owe all that I have" (qtd. in Pope vi). Although there is one obscure story about Bierce reading his father's copy of *The Iliad*, and his father's library was rumored to be the largest collection of books in the county, no one knows for sure what titles he owned. Given that Marcus A. Bierce was the offspring of five generations of orthodox Calvinists and had himself been a member of a congregation whose pastor was an understudy of Jonathan Edwards, surely both the Bible and *The Pilgrim's Progress* would have been an important part of his library. Because this is what Ambrose Bierce had grown up with, it is not surprising to find it richly influencing his stories of the war's early days. Exactly how much Bible reading Bierce did in his early years is difficult to determine. In a letter written in early 1913, he claimed, "I have read that book from cover to cover three times, and am in the habit of reading it now—it is a very interesting book" (*Misunderstood* 229).

Associating West Virginia with Bunyan's pilgrim was something Bierce did for the rest of his life.[5] In a letter he wrote shortly before his 1903 visit to the West Virginia battlefields, he wrote:

> The element of enchantment in that forest is supplied by my wandering and dreaming in it forty-one years ago when I was a-soldering and there were new things under a new sun. It is miles away, but from a near-by summit I can overlook the entire region—ridge beyond ridge, parted by purple valleys full of sleep [. . .]. Can you guess my feelings when I view this Dream-land—my Realm of Adventure? [. . .] I shall go; I shall retrace my old routes and lines of march; stand in my old camps; inspect my battlefields to see all is right and undisturbed. I shall go to the Enchanted Forest. (*Letters* 204)

A similar tone is evident in a regimental reunion letter written some forty years after the war. Bierce claimed that in West Virginia "there are neither enemies nor victories, but only glorious mountains and sleepy valleys all aflame with autumn foliage [. . .] hazy and dim as old memories" (*Battlefields* 3). It seems that the primary literary influences the young soldier brought with him from home forever became the means by which he attempted to express his fondness for his first real military posting.

So strong an association between the two further illuminates why Bierce would use such unspecific settings for "A Tough Tussle" or "The Mocking-Bird," and such a specific one for "A Horseman in the Sky." In the former, there is no need for a specific topographic feature, and the general and somewhat hazy memories of a private soldier almost thirty years earlier suffice to tell the story. In the case of the latter, one in which a very specific piece of land is critical, even a brief pass by the Tuscarora Cliffs would leave such an impression on a private from Indiana that he could recall its basic features years later. Inaccuracies in details such as roads could be a result of fading memory, having a limited view in the first place, necessary fictional modifications, or, most likely, a combination of all three.

First, as a private performing sentry duties like those of William Grayrock and Carter Druse and, later in the campaign, as a sergeant performing such duties as being "in command of a detachment of men constituting a picket-guard" like Lieutenant Byring, Ambrose Bierce never exceeds the military, historical, or geographic limits of his own experience in West Virginia (III: 106). It is a model that would serve him in nineteen other war stories as well.

Chapter 3

Midwar Stories

1862, Shiloh to the Railroad

I have got to die tomorrow morning—to be
hanged by the Federals. Mother, do not grieve
for me. I must bid you good-by forevermore.
Mother, I do not fear to die.

Sam Davis
convicted spy, November 1863

HEMP, *n.* A plant from whose fibrous bark is made
an article of neckwear which is frequently put on
after public speaking in the open air and prevents
the wearer from taking cold.
POLITICIAN, *n.* An eel in the fundamental mud
upon which the superstructure of organized
society is reared.

The Devil's Dictionary

A truck picked me up, and for the first time in
my life, someone called me "sir." The driver said,
"Where are you going, sir?" I told him north,
and that I'd been a sergeant up until a few minutes ago, so don't call me "sir." "Yes, sir," he
replied, and we roared down the road.

Lieutenant David Hackworth
About Face (1989)

Formative as the time in West Virginia was for the soldiers from Indiana, the carnage at Shiloh, Tennessee, in early April 1862 was even more so. Shiloh was the ninth costliest battle of the war, with combined casualties estimated at 23,741 killed, wounded, or missing. The heavy casualties were due in large part to Generals Grant and Sherman's lackadaisical security measures as their army lay in camp at Pittsburg Landing, Tennessee. Sherman confidently estimated that there was no enemy nearer than Corinth, Mississippi, some twenty-three miles away. At dawn on April 6, General Albert Sidney Johnston's Confederate force of 44,000 attacked the unsuspecting Union encampment. Bierce makes a narrative aside of sorts in "The Mocking-Bird" to explain that "many of Grant's men when spitted on Confederate bayonets were as naked as civilians; but it should be allowed that this was not because of any defect in their picket line. The error was of another sort: they had no pickets" (II: 219). Grant immediately called for help from General Don Carlos Buell's army. Buell's force included General William Nelson's division, of which Hazen's Brigade was a part, then about ten miles away from Pittsburg Landing. The force of Johnston's initial attack literally pinned the Union forces with their backs to the Tennessee River. With the help from Buell, however, the Union forces were able to drive the Confederates into a retreat toward Corinth late on April 7. As Morris and several other historians have noted, "Both sides were effectively in shock from the unparalleled bloodletting" of the first day's battle, and by the end of the second, more Americans would die than in the Revolutionary War, War of 1812, and Mexican War combined (Morris 34).

General Hazen and, one suspects, consequently, Sergeant Bierce never overcame the negative opinions they formed of Grant and the positive ones they formed of Buell as a result of the battle at Shiloh Church. Even in stories such as "The Mocking-Bird" that have no significant connections to the battle, Bierce takes several pointed digs at Grant for "manifest incompetence" on April 6, 1862 (II: 150).

Another story with a prominent jab at Grant is "Two Military Executions" (1906), one of Bierce's last Civil War stories and representative of a time in his career when his short fiction lapsed into potboiler ghost stories for *Cosmopolitan*. It is the tale of Bennett Story Greene, a private executed by firing squad for striking an officer, Lieutenant Will Dudley. The two are old schoolmates and no one saw the striking incident, but a sense of duty compelled the young lieutenant to report the breech of discipline. Dudley visits Greene on the eve of his execution and asks his forgiveness, to which Greene refuses a reply. A few weeks later, during the hard fighting at Shiloh, the company first sergeant forms the unit for a roll call and accidentally calls Greene's name. To everyone's surprise, a voice answers. Twice the captain orders the name called again, and each time the voice of Greene answers. Then a single shot rings out from afar. The captain exclaims, "What the devil does it mean?" Lieutenant Dudley comes forward from behind the formation, opens his coat to reveal a chest wound, exclaims, "It means this," and falls dead (III: 365).

In a now predictable pattern, Bierce sets the story in a historical context that is not only accurate but one he personally experienced. The tale opens with a description of Buell's army in camp. It is "a raw, untrained army, although some of its factions had seen hard enough service, with a good deal of fighting, in the mountains of Western Virginia, and in Kentucky" (III: 361). Not long after the execution of Private Greene, his former unit is "ferried over the Tennessee River to assist in succoring Grant's beaten army" after the first day at Shiloh, exactly as happened to the Ninth Indiana and Hazen's Brigade (III: 362–63).

However, it is not the accuracy of the setting that is particularly important. Of greater significance in this otherwise inferior military ghost story is the thematic concern with military discipline and the relationship between seniors and subordinates. According to the narrator, "To one imbued from infancy with the fascinating fallacy that all men are born equal, unquestioning submission to authority is not easily mastered and the American volunteer soldier in his 'green and salad days' is among the worst known" (III: 361). Doubtless with the two-word pun on the young soldier's name intended, Ben Greene "committed the indiscretion of striking his officer. Later in the war he would not have done that" (III: 361). Instead of responding by thrashing Greene, which is what the private claims Dudley used to do to him in school, Dudley reports the incident, and a court-martial sentences Greene to be shot. The last words that Greene speaks to Dudley are "Nobody saw me strike you; discipline would not have suffered much" (III: 362). Here seems to be the crux of the matter: how to reconcile old relationships with the dramatic new conditions imposed by military discipline and necessity. The issue doubtless concerned Sergeant Bierce in late 1861 and early 1862, especially in light of the fact that the Ninth Indiana had become a part of disciplinarian William B. Hazen's brigade in February. Only six months before Shiloh, Bierce had been promoted to sergeant-major and became the top noncommissioned officer in Company C of the Ninth Indiana. One must remember that in volunteer regiments, soldiers from the same town or area typically mustered in together to form the unit.

Company C, for example, at the beginning of the war consisted overwhelmingly of volunteers from Elkhart and Elkhart County. Many of these newly minted soldiers had known each other long before they enlisted, and the basic scenario of "Two Military Executions," that of friends now separated by military rank, was an issue with which many struggled.

Bierce recasts this struggle in "The Coup de Grâce" (1889), another story that appears connected with the Battle of Shiloh. Here, then, is significant additional evidence that issues involving rank and its impact on relationships were much on Bierce's mind at the time. In "The Coup de Grâce," Captain Downing Madwell administers the death stroke to his company mate and closest boyhood friend, Sergeant Caffal Halcrow. Halcrow has not only been badly wounded, but mauled by foraging wild hogs before Madwell decides to bring his friend's suffering to an end.

Several features of the story seem to suggest West Virginia locations. As critics note, an actual incident of wild hogs mutilating the dead and dying appears in Bierce's 1909 West Virginia memoir "On a Mountain." The memoir concludes with a description of a winter day during which the Ninth Regiment came upon some Union corpses that were in different positions than they had been when the regiment passed them the day before. The soldiers at the head of the column quickly discover that "a heard of galloping swine" had been feasting on the bodies (I: 233). As a result, one might claim that "The Coup de Grâce" is set in West Virginia. Other evidence, however, strongly indicates that it is not. The general time of the action of "The Coup de Grâce" is clear enough. The narrator claims, "The art of repartee was cultivated in military circles as early as 1862" (II: 127). By February 1862, the Ninth Indiana was out of West Virginia and in Tennessee, which makes a West Virginia setting unlikely. There are no geographic clues as to the location of the story; however, it does follow a major battle—something that never occurred while the Ninth was in West Virginia.

As in the West Virginia stories, battlefield circumstances physically isolate the protagonist from other individuals while he must make a critical moral decision. In a typical Biercean twist, Madwell, having used his last bullet to put a wounded horse out of its misery, must run his own saber through his boyhood friend's heart to end Halcrow's suffering. Just as Madwell finishes his grim task and Halcrow dies, Halcrow's brother, a major in the regiment, appears with a team of stretcher bearers intending to take the wounded man to the hospital.

In other Bierce war stories, son kills father, brother kills brother, and husband kills wife. In all of those, the parties involved are on opposite sides of the conflict. Here, however, friend kills close friend, and not only are both soldiers in the same regiment, they are even in the same company. Certainly the moral question of whether Madwell did the right thing by euthanizing Halcrow is the central question in the story, yet there is another important issue at work. As close as Madwell and Halcrow are, there is a division between them that, in some respects, puts the two at odds. Although it might seem like little more than an interesting side note to many readers, just as in "Two Military Executions," the issue of rank is quite significant in this story and adds an important dimension to the action.

Madwell and Halcrow grew up together and were the closest of friends. Halcrow even enlisted in the company in which Madwell was a lieutenant not because he wanted to be a soldier but because he wanted to stay close to his friend. The two are promoted in the course of the war, Madwell to captain and Halcrow to sergeant. "But," as the narrator explains, "between the highest non-commissioned and the lowest commissioned officer the gulf is deep and wide and the old relation was maintained with difficulty and a difference" (II: 125). Shortly before that, the narrator also comments, "In so far as disparity in rank, difference in duties and considerations of military discipline would permit they were commonly together" (II: 125). At a time when many commanding officers did indeed have the authority to order the summary executions of their soldiers for certain offenses, to have Madwell the officer mercifully execute Halcrow the noncommissioned officer is another of Bierce's characteristically macabre complications. To add yet another, Caffal Halcrow's older brother Creede, whom Madwell abhors and vice versa, is a major in the regiment and thus outranks Madwell. In light of this, one is left wondering if the executioner will, in turn, himself be executed.

Just what the "difference" the disparity in rank creates in the Madwell/Halcrow friendship, the narrator leaves to the reader's imagination. Certainly the gulf between the two ranks is aptly identified, but not adequately accounted for or explained. For all the difficulty of describing the experience of combat, describing the subtle nuances of the officer/enlisted relationship, as Bierce discovers here, is almost as difficult. The "difficulty and distance" between the ranks is something of which Bierce himself was acutely aware. Such an awareness came not simply with his own relatively rapid rise to the rank of sergeant-major, "the highest non-commissioned officer." It would be intensified when, on December 1, 1862, the commander of C Company promoted him to second lieutenant, and thus Bierce himself crossed the gulf to "the lowest commissioned officer" rank.

Three weeks later the *Elkhart Review*, the regiment's hometown paper, ran a column about "certain grievances" aired in a letter from a member of the company. According to the editor:

> The first complaint made is that an individual very obnoxious to the Company has been recommended for the 2nd Lieutenancy, and that, too, after repeated promises that no person should be commissioned who was not elected by a majority of the votes of the Company. ("Complaint")

Bierce wrote the *Review* in response, claiming that he had been done a "great injustice" by the printed letters. The paper responded with an editorial that attempted to balance the issues claiming that

> Lieut. Bierce has earned a reputation for daring and discipline that he may well be proud of, but we would not justify him in wrongdoing the men under his command if he possessed the skill and courage of Napoleon Bonapart [*sic*]; neither do we desire to detract one iota from his well-earned laurels. ("We have been shown")

In the early part of the war, promotion within the ranks of volunteer regiments was often by popular vote. As the war continued and casualties mounted in such costly battles as Antietam and Shiloh, that practice gave way to the realization that, as in the regular Army, meritocracy, not democracy, tended to save lives and win battles. The following week the *Review* published a letter from a Sergeant W. J. Chapman of C Company that indicated the grievances had been found without foundation. Of Bierce's promotion, Chapman wrote (emphasis as in original): "As to Lieut. Bierce's appointment it was *not* the *man* we complained of,—the Lieut. has always been a good and brave soldier, and *knows no fear*, but it was being deprived of the privilege of election by ballot" ("Act of Justice"). Thus the internal controversy surrounding his promotion only added to the significance of this benchmark event.

Important as the issue of rank was to Lieutenant Bierce in 1862, the more fundamental concern of "The Coup de Grâce," the ethics of mercy killing, certainly crossed his mind as well. As mentioned earlier, there are no significant geographical indications of the location of the story. Although the wild pigs incident appears in a West Virginia memoir, if Bierce is true to his habit of setting the action of his stories at the same time he was at the place, then dating the story in 1862 rules out West Virginia as a location. Another memoir, however, strongly suggests a solution to the question of location.

At the outset of "The Coup de Grâce," crews of stretcher bearers are working to remove the wounded and bury the dead, of which there are many. In fact, "[a]s far as one could see through the forests, among the splintered trees, lay wrecks of men and horses" (II: 122). The extent of the carnage and the mention of the year 1862 suggest that the story could be based on the battle at Shiloh. Bierce's 1881 memoir "What I Saw of Shiloh" strongly reinforces that possibility. Running some thirty-five pages, it is by far the longest of the memoirs and, at times, seems a tour of battlefield grotesqueries. The graphic descriptions of the dead in the short story roughly echo those in the memoir. The story, for example, explains: "The dead were collected in groups of a dozen or a score and laid side by side in rows" (II: 122), and the memoir states: "But there was a very pretty line of dead continually growing in our rear, and doubtless the enemy had at his back a similar encouragement" (I: 258). There are no wild pigs in "What I Saw of Shiloh," but, as in "The Coup de Grâce," there is a memorable and frequently quoted encounter with a badly wounded Federal sergeant. Bierce and his troops find the non-commissioned officer who is breathing convulsively and sputtering blood:

> A bullet had clipped a groove in his skull, above the temple; from this the brain protruded in bosses, dropping off in flakes and strings. [. . .] One of my men whom I knew for a womanish fellow, asked if he should put his bayonet through him. Inexpressibly shocked by the cold-blooded proposal, I told him I thought not; it was unusual, and too many were looking. (I: 255)

Here then is an analogue for the situation described in "The Coup de Grâce." They are alike in several fundamentals: a badly wounded sergeant, a decision to make about killing him, and the use of an edged weapon, as opposed to a firearm, to do the job.[1] Fortunately, Sergeant Major Bierce did not make the same decision as Captain Madwell.

As if to confirm that the battlefield at Shiloh inspired the events of "The Coup de Grâce," both memoir and story conclude with the appearance of three men, two of whom are medical staff. Following the men's arrival, a short declarative sentence concludes each piece:

> See; here comes a stretcher-bearer, and there a surgeon! Good heavens! a chaplain!
> The battle was indeed at an end. (I: 268)

> At that moment three men stepped silently forward from behind the clump of young trees which had concealed their approach. Two were hospital attendants and carried a stretcher.
> The third was Major Creede Halcrow. (II: 132)

Here the memoir adds a significant insight into the story. Certainly in both, the battle itself was indeed at an end. In the story, however, a second battle, the long-standing feud between Madwell and Creede Halcrow, is also at an end. While the chaplain of the memoir might be one entrusted to render moral judgment on the situation, Creede Halcrow, as mentioned earlier, cannot only render such judgment but see to it that it is carried out on the hapless Madwell.

Issues of rank and duty were not the only concerns on Ambrose Bierce's mind as he advanced his military career in early 1862. The war was also a time when he was becoming all too aware of the workings of American politics and politicians. Two more Bierce war stories, both with connections to Shiloh, highlight the young soldier's increasing awareness of the types of political machinations that would later so often be the subject of his newspaper editorializing. "Jupiter Doke, Brigadier-General" (1885), set in late 1861 and early 1862, tells the story of a scheming small-town politician who receives an appointment to the rank of brigadier and bumbles his way into history. For reasons that will become apparent, this story will be discussed in a later chapter. The second story concerning politicians in 1862 is "An Affair of Outposts" (1897). As in "Two Military Executions" and "The Coup de Grâce," Bierce voices his criticism of General Grant and praises Don Carlos Buell. Here, the outspoken narrator of "An Affair of Outposts" claims, "For manifest incompetence Grant, whose beaten army had been saved from destruction and capture by Buell's soldierly activity and skill, had been relieved of his command" (II: 150).[2] But the central antagonist of the story is not a general but a state governor, a governor based on a figure with whom Bierce was quite familiar.

"An Affair of Outposts" opens with a state governor reluctantly granting an officer's commission to a Mr. Armisted, whom the governor knows to be of divided loyalties and questionable motives. The young man's motive is that he wishes to die because his wife is having an affair with an unknown suitor. Months later, in the wake of Shiloh, the governor makes a battlefield visit to troops of his state as they pursue the Confederates toward Corinth. He visits the unit that the now battle-hardened and prematurely aged Captain Armisted commands. Armisted and many of his men die in a skirmish while protecting the governor. As a doctor treats the governor for a twisted ankle, the governor picks up a folded piece of paper that had fallen from Armisted's pocket during the melee. It is a letter from Armisted's wife expressing "the penitence of a faithless wife deserted by her betrayer" (II: 163). The governor quietly transfers the letter to his own pocket, the clear implication being that he is the woman's betrayer.

There can be little doubt that Bierce had Oliver P. Morton, wartime governor of Indiana, in mind when he wrote "An Affair of Outposts." Morton was himself a controversial figure, but how accurately the fictional governor of "An Affair of Outposts" represents the actual governor is difficult to assess. Like the fictional governor, Morton visited battlefields, including Shiloh, where Indiana regiments had recently fought or were fighting. Physically, the fictional governor is, like Morton, "too fat to hop" (II: 156). More importantly, both governors ardently support the war effort. In "An Affair of Outposts," the narrator explains that in 1861 the fictional governor was "already famous for the intelligence and zeal with which he directed all the powers and resources of his State to the service of the Union" (II: 146). Whether his motives were primarily political or more altruistic, Morton's involvement in the war effort was extensive. He was instrumental in raising regiments for the Union early in the war, and the response from the state was truly impressive. Indiana ranked second in percentage of eligible men who served in the Union army. Morton also established a system of medical care and long-term support for wounded Indiana soldiers. He carried on personal negotiations with Confederate authorities in Richmond during the winter of 1863 in order to get blankets and rations delivered to Indiana prisoners of war (Thornbrough 168). According to historian Emma Thornbrough, "The Governor cherished and deserved the name of 'soldier's friend'" (169). One soldier in the Army of the Cumberland wrote home, "You ought to hear the shouts of the soldiers from all states whenever Governor Morton is mentioned" (qtd. in Thornbrough 169). All of this rings true with the fictional governor, whom Bierce describes as "[a]t the headquarters of the army and in the camps of the troops from his State [. . .] a familiar figure" (II: 150–51). Yet one must wonder why such an ostensibly laudatory figure might inspire such an unflattering fictional counterpart.

Commendable as Morton sounds, one can imagine the problems his good intentions could create for a commander like General Hazen with a brigade composed of units from several states: if the Indiana troops appeared to be receiving special treatment or an inequitable share of comfort items, then morale in other regiments would suffer. At times, having high-ranking civilian political visitors could become a real hindrance to the conduct of tactical operations due to the time spent attending to them and the drain on unit manpower caused by the visitors' constant need for added protection and security around battlefield areas, a point the events of "An Affair of Outposts" illustrates well.

Yet General Hazen never took Morton to task, at least not in print. He mentions Morton only once in *A Narrative of Military Service*, commenting that the very cantankerous and outspoken General William Nelson "had taken a violent dislike to Indiana [. . .] and to all people who came from it. Excepting Governor Morton, of whom he always spoke in the highest praise" (56). Any conjecture about Hazen's feelings toward Morton is difficult, however, because when Morton made his post-Shiloh battlefield visit, Hazen was convalescing from a case of malaria and was not in the field.

"An Affair of Outposts" and the farcical "Jupiter Doke, Brigadier-General" reflect their author's growing awareness of and concerns with politics and politicians in the early months of 1862. The battle at Shiloh and Oliver Morton's postbattle visit certainly pressed home the contemporary ramifications of civilian control of the military to Sergeant Ambrose Bierce.

The events at Shiloh were also the prelude to the fall of Corinth, Mississippi, which, in turn, focused much of the Army of the Cumberland's attentions on the railroads of Mississippi, Tennessee, and Alabama. These rail lines were to provide the backdrop for the war story that has largely kept Bierce's name alive for generations of readers.

"A man stood on a railroad bridge in northern Alabama," begins Ambrose Bierce's most famous and most anthologized short story, "An Occurrence at Owl Creek Bridge" (1890). Critics generally regard this tale as Bierce at his best. It is a paramount example of literary impressionism in which extraordinary psychological stresses alter a character's perception of the external world. Critical to the story's success, and the subject of much scholarly work about it, is the reader's willingness to accept without question the character's distorted sensory input.[3] Bierce follows his penchant for blending personal experience, actual terrain, and accurate history to create the quality of verisimilitude, a key to accomplishing this reader complicity.

"An Occurrence at Owl Creek Bridge" describes the hanging of Peyton Farquhar, a southern planter caught attempting to sabotage a railroad bridge considered vital by the Union army. From the outset, Bierce clearly locates the action of the story in Alabama. He reinforces the historical accuracy of the setting with a brief reference to the fall of Corinth, an immediate consequence of the Battle of Shiloh. However, there is an important fictional modification in the geography of the setting. Owl Creek is in Tennessee, not northern Alabama. Slightly more than a mile west of Shiloh Church is the terrain feature that became the western boundary of the battlefield: Owl Creek—a well-known locale because for many of the Union soldiers encamped near the church, it had been a place to bathe and swim before the battle.

"An Occurrence at Owl Creek Bridge" first appeared in the *San Francisco Examiner* on July 13, 1890. Although set in a location Bierce left nearly twenty-five years earlier, his intimate knowledge of terrain and railroads in northern Alabama and southern Tennessee, and his participation in the battle of Shiloh, rule out a simple geographical mistake when he placed Owl Creek in Alabama. Only one critic, Edmund Wilson, has noted that Bierce, "transposed the Owl Creek from Tennessee to Alabama," but Wilson does not elaborate beyond that brief comment (618). Bierce's transposition of the creek was surely deliberate and, given his preoccupation with topography, not just a coincidental use of a creek by the same name as the one near Shiloh.

Just how familiar Bierce was with northern Alabama is not difficult to establish. His postwar experiences as a treasury agent took him all over that part of the state. Prior to that, in October 1864, as a topographic engineer, he was in northeastern Alabama along the Coosa River. By late November, Bierce had moved on horseback with General Schofield's army through north central Alabama into southern Tennessee directly along the route of the Tennessee and Alabama Railroad line, which was also known as the Central Alabama Railroad. Even earlier than that, in late July, 1862, General Hazen records in his memoir, "After remaining a few weeks at Athens [Alabama], and passing a month in repairing the Nashville Southern Railroad, the brigade took post at Murfreesboro" (*Narrative* 51). It appears here that Hazen mistakenly recorded the name of another railroad that connects with the Tennessee and Alabama Line, because official records indicate that the Ninth Indiana was posted along the Tennessee and Alabama Line in June and July 1862. If Bierce is here true to his practice of casting the action of his war stories during the same time period that he was at the place he writes about, one must wonder which of the three times that he was in northern Alabama the Owl Creek Bridge story draws upon. Bierce himself answers the question clearly. The original newspaper version of the story begins, "One morning in the summer of 1862 a man stood upon a railroad bridge in Northern Alabama."[4] It was a line that he would edit for the version of the story that appeared in *Tales of Soldiers and Civilians*.

Assuming, for the moment, that Bierce was set on using Owl Creek as the name of the body of water under his fatal bridge, the obvious question is why did he not simply move the story to Owl Creek,

Tennessee. The simplest answer is that there is no railroad there. Although the outcome at Shiloh was the vital step for eventual Union control of the rail center at Corinth farther to the south, the nearest railroad was twenty-three miles from the Shiloh battlefield (Turner 126). With railroads so few in the South, any readers of Bierce's day and later who were familiar with the basic geography of the area would be far more likely to remember that there is no railroad over Owl Creek, Tennessee, than to simply accept without question a creek by that name crossed by an existing railroad in Alabama. After all, there are many small creeks in northern Alabama. Although this is a sufficient and satisfactory explanation for this most notable of Bierce's topographic twists, a more detailed explanation of the geographic and historical context serves to better illuminate Bierce's thinking.

During the Civil War, there were only two rail lines through northern Alabama. The Tennessee and Alabama line split northern Alabama in two from the north and terminated at Decatur. The Memphis and Charleston line ran east and west across the northern portion of the state and connected with the Tennessee and Alabama line at Decatur (map 5). Detailed topographic maps along the routes of the Tennessee and Alabama line and the Memphis and Charleston line verify that neither cross an Owl Creek located in Alabama. Bierce did not use an actual Alabama creek name that, by coincidence, was the same as the creek near Shiloh.

Finally, if one recalls that Shiloh led to Corinth and Corinth led to the railroads, one quickly realizes that Owl Creek at Shiloh in Tennessee,

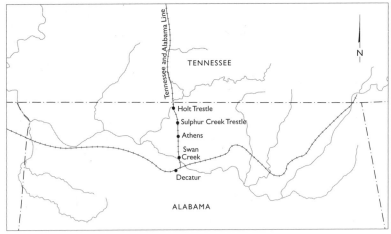

Map 5. Northern Alabama, showing Confederate railroads.

and the Tennessee and Alabama Railroad in Alabama very roughly mark the western and eastern boundaries respectively of an important campaign for Hazen's Brigade and the Ninth Indiana Volunteers. Shiloh is twenty-three miles from Corinth; Corinth is eighty-five miles from the railroad in northern Alabama. For Bierce to identify strongly with the two terrain features that provide a longitudinal geographic frame for an important phase of the war and to have brought the two together in one story, much as he did with the cliff in "A Horseman in the Sky," is entirely consistent with his demonstrated craft choices.

Historically, the northern Alabama setting is especially appropriate. Not only was Bierce engaged in repairing the Tennessee and Alabama line in the summer of 1862, in late September of 1864, shortly before Bierce's return to that railroad, Confederate General Nathan Bedford Forrest's cavalry destroyed many critical sections of the Tennessee and Alabama line again to deny the Union army use of it. Forrest began just north of the heavy Union defenses at the Decatur junction. He attacked the Federal garrison at Athens, Alabama, on September 23 and "was able to destroy nearly all of the bridges and trestles on the Tennessee and Alabama Railroad between Decatur and Spring Hill" (Sword 77). Forrest captured, destroyed, and then quickly withdrew from a fortified Union post at the Sulphur Branch Trestle in what was one of the last Confederate victories of the war.

In "An Occurrence at Owl Creek Bridge," Peyton Farquhar has been biding his time since the fall of Corinth. A Federal scout, disguised as a Confederate soldier, tells Farquhar, "The Yanks are repairing the railroads [. . .] and are getting ready for another advance. They have reached the Owl Creek bridge, put it in order and built a stockade on the north bank" (II: 33). Farquhar asks, "Is there no force on this side of the creek?" Farquhar implies that he is on the south side of the creek. Later in the story, Union artillery fires from near the bridge on Farquhar as he attempts to escape by swimming up the creek. Given actual events of Bierce's unit's repairing the line in 1862 and of Forrest's raids in late 1864, a fictional story set along the Tennessee and Alabama Railroad fits the historical scenario precisely.

Geographic hints in the story also support locating "Owl Creek Bridge" on the Tennessee and Alabama Railroad. Farquhar's exchange with the Federal scout describes a railroad running north and south through northern Alabama and a creek running east and west. During the War, there was only one such north-south railroad, the Tennessee and Alabama. The route of the Tennessee and Alabama line from the

Tennessee border to Decatur, Alabama, had three locations with a north–south railroad bridge spanning an east–west creek. They are Holt Trestle on Mill Creek just north of Elkmont; Sulphur Creek Trestle south of Elkmont; and Swan Creek between Tanner and Rowland (map 5). The span at Holt Creek was very short and not heavily garrisoned, not a plausible location for the story. The long trestle at Sulphur Creek, however, not only spanned an east–west creek, it had a stockaded Union blockhouse on the north bank, was garrisoned primarily with troops from the Ninth Indiana Cavalry (not to be confused with Bierce's Ninth Indiana Infantry) and was protected by artillery.[5] After Forrest's raid, the trestle and stockade were put back in order, exactly the same sort of situation as the disguised Federal scout in "Owl Creek Bridge" explains to the unsuspecting Farquhar.

In summary, Bierce's northern Alabama setting coincides with his personal experience, larger historical events, and actual topography, most specifically with the Sulphur Creek Trestle that Bierce was known to have visited just two months after it briefly fell into Confederate hands. The fact that a cavalry regiment from Indiana manned the trestle makes it all the more likely that Bierce, in his trip up the line in 1864, would stop to talk with soldiers from his home state about the recent fighting there. The scenario in "An Occurrence at Owl Creek Bridge" is most likely a conflation inspired by events of both 1862 and 1864. Here again, one sees Bierce remaining faithful not only to the larger historical context but to the very local one as well.

Because a hanging is at the center of the story, one might wonder if Bierce witnessed an event similar to the one described in "An Occurrence at Owl Creek Bridge." He did not. In very late 1862 or very early 1863, about the time of Bierce's commissioning, he witnessed a double hanging near Murfreesboro. The hanging was an internal disciplinary matter for the Union army—two of its soldiers were hanged in front of the troops for a particularly brutal murder. Bierce retold the story in *The Argonaut* in 1878. He noted that a railroad engineer on a track near the scaffold whistled a seemingly mocking "Hoot! Hoot!" with his engine when one of the convicted men began to exclaim that he was "going home to Jesus" (21 Dec. 78).

However, the central events of "Owl Creek Bridge" may well have analogues not so much in things Bierce witnessed, but in ones that he personally experienced. In October 1864, Bierce was a Confederate prisoner in northeastern Alabama for four days. He recorded his experiences in a memoir entitled "Four Days in Dixie" (1888). Fortunately for

Bierce, his captors were not especially competent, and as they evacuated him to their higher headquarters, he managed to escape while the party slept in an isolated farmhouse.

The record of his brief captivity contains several revealing comments. In the moments immediately before the enemy discovers and begins pursuing him, Bierce sees some Confederate cavalry on a nearby hill: "On this crest suddenly appeared two horsemen in gray, sharply outlined against the sky—men and animals looking gigantic. [. . . In moments] the giants on the crest had multiplied" (I: 301). Bierce flees into a swamp where, he writes, "Finding myself unpursued after the lapse of what seemed an hour, but was probably a few minutes, I cautiously sought a place where, still concealed, I could obtain a view" (I: 302). What is especially significant about these passages is the sensory distortion that Bierce records himself experiencing. Peyton Farquhar has similar experiences of distortion of both vision and time. As Farquhar stands with his neck in the noose looking down at the creek below he "let his gaze wander to the swirling water of the stream racing madly beneath his feet. A piece of dancing driftwood caught his attention and his eyes followed it down the current. How slowly it appeared to move! What a sluggish stream!" (II: 30). Shortly thereafter, time becomes dilated in much the same way Bierce experienced:

> he became conscious of a new disturbance. Striking through the thought of his dear ones was a sound [. . .] like the stroke of a blacksmith's hammer upon the anvil [. . .]. Its recurrence was regular, but as slow as the tolling of a death knell. He awaited each stroke with impatience [. . .]. The intervals of silence grew progressively longer; the delays became maddening. With their greater infrequency the sounds increased in strength [. . .]. What he heard was the ticking of his watch. (II: 31)

Farquhar is one of several protagonists who experience sensory distortion that, albeit far more pronounced, is consistent with what Bierce reports in "Four Days in Dixie." Carter Druse of "A Horseman in the Sky," for example, upon first awakening and seeing his father on the cliff "magnified by its lift against the sky" perceives that horse and rider appear "of heroic, almost colossal size" (II: 20). Even more than what Farquhar experiences, Druse's resonates very strongly with Bierce's own report that the enemy "outlined against the sky—men and animals looked gigantic" in the moments before his capture. Here again it is entirely consistent with his methods for Bierce to draw on sensations he was familiar with to add verisimilitude to the profound sensory distortion Farquhar experiences.

The memoir also confirms that hanging was on the young Bierce's mind at the time of his capture. As southern soldiers escorted Bierce to their headquarters miles away, his guards expressed genuine concerns about encountering Confederate guerrillas. As Bierce relates:

> if we should chance to meet Jeff Gatewood he would probably take me from them and hang me to the nearest tree; and once or twice, hearing horsemen approach, they directed me to stand aside, concealed in the brush, one of them remaining near by to keep an eye on me [. . .].
>
> Jeff Gatewood was a 'guerrilla' chief of local notoriety [. . .]. My guards related almost incredible tales of his cruelties and infamies. (I: 310)

Certainly this passage suggests that the hanging in "An Occurrence at Owl Creek Bridge" may have been much more the result of something Bierce came perilously close to personally experiencing than of an event he witnessed.

Unfortunately, any attempt to explain why Bierce chose to borrow "Owl Creek" rather than use an actual Alabama creek name is fraught with speculation. However, two important considerations emerge. The first concerns verisimilitude, that quality of believability that Bierce deftly creates in this story. Much as in "A Horseman in the Sky," to locate the story clearly at the Sulphur Creek Trestle is to risk discovery. That is to say, a reader already familiar with either the history or terrain (or both) is likely to know that no such hanging actually occurred on the bridge. Such a reader will probably also know that, as large as the trestle was, the stream underneath it is small, hardly enough to wade in, let alone swim. A not-so-knowledgeable, but curious, reader could research Sulphur Creek's history with relative ease and make the same discoveries. As it is, Bierce's historiography and renamed terrain feature sufficiently obscure the setting so as to leave the reader once again asking, "I wonder if that really happened?"

A fairly straightforward reading of the story not only suggests a second possible reason Bierce would alter geography but also highlights how "Owl Creek Bridge" further documents Bierce's development as a soldier. Peyton Farquhar is a romantic, idealistic man. Etymologically, his surname itself means both "brave man of noble descent" and "gray clad man" (Ames 67, Cheatham and Cheatham 45). Farquhar, the narrator explains, longs for "the larger life of the soldier, the opportunity for distinction." There was "No service was too humble for him to perform in aid of the South, no adventure too perilous." He is "at heart a soldier" (II: 32–33). His entire escape sequence is a romantic fantasy. Farquhar's emergence from underwater is a romantic birth image: "He felt his head emerge; his eyes were blinded by the sunlight; his chest expanded convulsively, and with a supreme and crowning agony his lungs engulfed a great draught of air, which instantly he expelled in a shriek!" (II: 37). Farquhar's death, like the wrecked riverboat *Walter Scott* in *Huckleberry Finn*, can be read as emblematic of the death of romanticism and its trappings. Here also, of course, is the demise of any sort of romanticism associated with the war.

Given such a reading, the owl becomes an important symbol. Traditionally, it is an emblem of darkness and death as well as wisdom. It is an especially appropriate one to associate with the scene of Farquhar's hanging because, ironically, Farquhar's insight into the true nature of war comes at the expense of his life, a motif Bierce uses again and again in his war stories. By the summer of 1862 the war had brought Bierce exactly the same sort of insight but, fortunately, without the same personal consequences. One sees a primary example of this reflected in Bierce reminiscing about the skirmish at Greenbrier River in late 1861: "This place had its battle—what was called a battle in the 'green and salad days' of the great rebellion" (XI: 395). Here, with a bit of mild derision, Bierce recalls the "halcyon days" of the West Virginia campaign compared with the massive bloodletting he was to be a part of commencing with the battle at Shiloh Church and continuing until late 1864. Doubtless by the time the Ninth Indiana helped repair the Tennessee and Alabama line in the summer of 1862, any romantic notions of "the larger life of the soldier" were as broken in Sergeant Bierce as Peyton Farquhar's neck.

By the end of 1862, the Ninth Indiana had been a part of Hazen's Brigade for ten months. The picture one gets of Bierce at the time of his commissioning, especially as reflected in *The Elkhart Review*, makes it relatively easy to see why Bierce was attracted to Hazen's style of leadership. Indeed it would not be long before the newly minted lieutenant in Company C, Ninth Regiment, found himself on the staff of the brigade commander, an event that would bring new concerns to the fiction of Ambrose Bierce.

Chapter 4

Midwar Stories

1863, Stone's River to Chickamauga and Missionary Ridge

[. . .] duty—ah, duty is as cruel as death!
Ambrose Bierce
"Three and One Are One" (1908)

Colonels will call together the officers of their
commands, and impress upon them the fact that
everything depends upon the proper perform-
ance of their duties, and that they must exercise
absolute power over their men, who are always
ready to do their duty.
William B. Hazen
A Narrative of Military Service

GHOST, *n.* The outward and visible sign of an
inward fear.
PROJECTILE, *n.* [. . .] With the growth of prudence
in military affairs the projectile came more and
more into favor, and is now held in high esteem
by the most courageous. Its capital defect is that
it requires personal attendance at the point of
propulsion.
The Devil's Dictionary

Possibly the [newspaper] correspondents have not
learned that the first and most elementary duty of
an officer in action is to keep his head on straight
and his heart out of his mouth.
Bierce
in the *San Francisco Examiner,* July 31, 1898

Hazen's Brigade spent virtually all of 1863 campaigning across southern Tennessee. Three battles provide the benchmark events of the year: Stone's River at Murfreesboro in January, Chickamauga in September, and Missionary Ridge in December. The year saw Second Lieutenant Ambrose Bierce promoted once again and moved to Hazen's staff and the all-important duties of topographic engineer. Certainly the young officer from Indiana had been growing at a rapid clip both personally and professionally during the first year and a half of the war, but 1863 would prove his most formative yet. His sheer literary output associated with the year is testimony to that fact—roughly half of Bierce's war stories are either set in or have important connections with events of 1863. Both his first two published war stories, "George Thurston" and "Jupiter Doke, Brigadier-General," and his very last, "Three and One Are One," have foundations in that year. However, numbers only tell part of the story. New themes evident in these stories reflect their author's growing professional maturity and the dramatically enlarged scope of his duties. The most prominent of these thematic concerns is with officership, that is, with the proper execution of the duties and responsibilities inherent in becoming a member of the commissioned ranks. Bierce also shows some refinements to and variations on his practice of writing about places where he had been, especially when telling a ghost story, as he was often want to do late in his career.

On the last day of 1862, the Ninth Indiana found itself in a battle that would prove more costly than Shiloh, yet one that has since been largely forgotten by the general public. The Battle of Stone's River, Tennessee, with its total casualties of 24,645, would be the eighth costliest of the war and Hazen's Brigade would play a critical role in the Union victory. The fighting at Stone's River was for control of Murfreesboro, about fifty miles south of Nashville. Advancing toward the city, the Army of the Cumberland clashed with Braxton Bragg's Army of Tennessee on December 31, just two miles northwest of the city where the Nashville Turnpike crossed the Nashville and Chattanooga Railroad. During the ensuing three days of fighting, Hazen's Brigade was at the center of the Union line, just north of the crossing in cotton fields that straddled both the tracks and the turnpike. The Union line to Hazen's right broke under repeated Confederate attacks and fell back along the Nashville road. Hazen's Brigade held its position and found itself at the apex of a V-shaped Union line. A history of the war published in 1868 claimed, "To Hazen's brigade is freely given the honor of saving the day, and perhaps the Army of the Cumberland. Thirteen hundred men, skillfully handled, had kept thousands at bay" (Lossing II: 547).

The newly commissioned Bierce fought in his infantry company during the battle of Stone's River and, as he had done in West Virginia, distinguished himself. This time he did it by carrying the Ninth's badly wounded acting commander, Major Branden, an Elkhart blacksmith, to safety under heavy enemy fire. Interestingly enough, years after the war Braden wrote that he always regarded Bierce as "cold and unapproachable" yet reported that when Bierce rescued him, both said what they thought would be final good-byes, and Bierce "was crying like a little girl" (qtd. in Richard O'Connor 30). In February, Bierce received a promotion to first lieutenant largely because of his bravery on the field at Stone's River. He had been a second lieutenant for just under three months.

In March, probably as a result of his distinguished record, he became a member of General Hazen's staff. He was initially assigned to the brigade staff as provost marshal, but within a few weeks became the acting topographer. In the meantime, Hazen's Brigade began a relatively long encampment at Readyville, Tennessee, about ten miles from the Stone's River battlefield.

If military service was the focal point of Bierce's early life, perhaps his entire life, then his duties as a topographic engineer were surely the center of his service. The stories he sets during his time as topographer are some of his most revealing. In them, one sees the young officer growing as a soldier. Now Bierce's military world would expand dramatically. No longer would the scope of his vision be largely confined to the world of Company C, Ninth Indiana Volunteers. As explained earlier, he would now occupy a key position in the brigade, and with both the added mobility of a horse and the ancillary duties expected of any staff officer, principally battlefield messenger and coordinator for the commander, Bierce's experiences and perspectives would extend even beyond the units within Hazen's Brigade. His stories set in this period reflect more complex themes of military leadership and what it means to be an officer. Although he never entirely forgets the concerns of private soldiers, these larger issues of leadership and command move to the thematic foreground.

Other changes as a result of his new position become evident as well. Beginning with the stories set in 1863 following his assumption of the duties of topographic engineer, Bierce will sometimes locate his stories clearly and unambiguously and modify neither the natural nor man-made features at all. This practice comes from an improved eye for such features and an ability to recall them years later, both the results of mapmaking. In the way that taking careful notes during a lecture helps one recall its content, making detailed maps of terrain helps one recall its features. Along with the mechanics of drawing a map itself, it is worthwhile here to recall Bierce's statement from "George Thurston" that clashes with the Confederates during mapping missions often "fixed in my memory a vivid and imperishable picture of the locality—a picture serving instead of accurate field notes" (II: 210–11).[1] Along with other evidence, because Bierce devotes much of the first two paragraphs of his first published war story to explaining the duties of the topographic engineer, it seems very reasonable to assert that these duties were central to his wartime experience.

Although "George Thurston" (1883) is Bierce's first published war story, "A Resumed Identity" (1908) is the piece of Bierce's Civil War fiction in which one can identify significant elements of the story that immediately follow his assumption of duties as Hazen's mapmaker. The action is postwar, but the tale is set in the context of the Battle of Stone's River, Tennessee. Typically, the story is rich in autobiographical parallels and is extremely accurate in both its historical context and the terrain of its setting.

Primarily a psychological tale, "A Resumed Identity" also has preternatural overtones. As the story opens, a soldier stands near a road on a summer night. He sees a long column of at least three infantry regiments along with cavalry and an artillery battery moving north on the road. He is struck by how quiet and spectral the figures appear in the moonlight. Sometime later, the soldier meets Dr. Stilling Malson of Murfreesboro returning on horseback from visiting a patient along the Nashville road. The soldier identifies himself as "a lieutenant, of the staff of General Hazen [. . .] [o]f the Federal army" (III: 179). He asks the doctor who won the battle and for directions to any part of the Union forces. The lieutenant claims he was superficially wounded in the battle and has been unconscious. Dr. Malson, somewhat perplexed, asks for his age and why he is in civilian clothes. Malson denies seeing any soldiers moving along the road. The lieutenant, angry at what he perceives to be an uncooperative attitude on the doctor's part, answers that he is twenty-three, tells the doctor to go to the devil, and walks away in disgust. As he wanders across the fields near the road, the lieutenant begins to realize that something is very wrong; he was fighting in late December, yet it is now summer. The lieutenant decides he must have spent several months in a hospital and has escaped to rejoin his unit. Shortly, he arrives at a small plot enclosed by a stone wall. In the center of the plot is "a square, solid monument of hewn stone" (III: 183). Catching a familiar name on one side of the monument, he leans over the wall and reads: "HAZEN'S BRIGADE To The Memory of Its Soldiers who fell at Stone River, Dec. 31,

1862" (III: 183). Taken aback at the sight of the inscription, the lieutenant crawls to a nearby pool of rainwater for a drink, looks at himself in it, and falls dead, face down in the pool.[2]

Bierce revisited the Stone's River battlefield in October 1907 while he and Percival Pollard were on a trip to Galveston, Texas. In a subsequent letter to George Sterling, Bierce wrote, "By the way, Pollard and I had a good time in Galveston and on the way I took him to some of my old battlefields" (*Letters* 142–43). McWilliams claims that "it was a memorable trip for Bierce. He paraded Pollard around the battlefield with a proprietary interest, pointing out monuments and delighting his guest with the quality of his reminiscences" (293). One prominent monument Bierce pointed out to Pollard was the one to Hazen's Brigade mentioned in "A Resumed Identity." The story made its first appearance less than one year later in the September 1908 issue of *Cosmopolitan*. The fact that Bierce's visit to the old battlefield preceded publication of the story is especially significant to McWilliams and Morris. Both biographers read the story as a sort of autobiographical allegory, a reading that would certainly explain the accuracy of its terrain and historical context but fails to account for some important points about the monument itself. McWilliams describes Bierce's 1907 visit to Stone's River:

> [Bierce] could read, through the dim unreality of twilight, the inscription on an elaborate monument in the center of the field. [. . .] It was like reading an inscription on his own tomb. It was such an amazing experience to stand on this field of death alone, that he suddenly felt all the sensations of the battle come surging over him [. . . and] he wrote "A Resumed Identity." [. . .] The experience, with its feeling of a lost reality, was genuine and personal. (46)

McWilliams and Morris view the tale as a sort of personal catharsis in which Bierce himself must be the nameless lieutenant who discovers how old he has grown after finding the monument. Implicit in McWilliams' comments is the notion that Bierce first saw the monument during his 1907 visit and was so moved by it that he wrote "A Resumed Identity." Although it certainly makes for a melodramatic vignette in a biography, this is an inadequate autobiographical interpretation. No doubt the monument was a primary inspiration for the story, and Bierce certainly required it as a device for the denouement; however, 1907 was not Bierce's initial encounter with the monument.

The soldiers of the brigade built the monument soon after the battle as a tribute to the approximately one-third of the brigade who were casualties. The monument stands on the site of the brigade's position during the battle and is at the center of a small plot surrounded by a stone wall. The soldiers constructed the wall of native Indiana limestone. Sixty-nine of Hazen's soldiers are buried within the small plot enclosed by the wall. The monument itself is ten feet square around the base and almost as high. Inscribed on all four sides, it commemorates those killed at Shiloh as well as Stone's River. The monument was erected in early 1863 while Hazen's Brigade was camped at Readyville, Tennessee, during the months of relative quiet that immediately followed the Stone's River battle (Lossing II: 546–47n and Hazen, *Narrative* 81, 94).

Within the brigade, the Ninth Indiana Volunteers were detailed to do the construction work on the monument (Lossing II: 546–47n, Hazen 81, 94). As a staff officer in the brigade, first provost marshal, then topographic engineer, throughout the building of the monument, Bierce had ample opportunity to view it during and immediately after construction. It was the first Civil War battlefield monument erected anywhere and was a center of attention for the entire brigade. Hazen's *A Narrative of Military Service*, which Bierce read sometime between 1885 and 1888, contains a full-page lithograph of the monument with the inscription quoted in "A Resumed Identity" clearly visible (fig. 1). By the time of his visit to the battlefield in 1907, Ambrose Bierce had seen the monument several times.

Fig. 1. Hazen's Monument at Stone's River. Lithograph from Hazen, *A Narrative of Military Service* (1885; Huntington, WV: Blue Acorn, 1993), facing p. 94.

If, as McWilliams reasonably conjectures, Bierce himself felt like the nameless lieutenant suddenly confronted with his own aged face, then the history of the Hazen Monument adds a subtle but very important dimension to his reading. It was not seeing the monument in 1907 that inspired the story; rather, it was seeing the changes in the monument since Bierce first saw it in the spring of 1863. Details of the appearance of the monument in "A Resumed Identity" give an autobiographical reading based on the history of the monument additional validity. When the lieutenant looks at the monument in the moonlight, "It was brown with age, weather-worn at the angles, spotted with moss and lichen. Between the massive blocks were strips of grass" (III: 183). This is much more like what the sixty-five-year-old Bierce saw in 1907 in contrast to the pristine faces of the monument he remembered from 1863. A parallel between the lieutenant discovering his aged face in the reflection made by the rainwater and Bierce himself now seems especially apropos.

With the highly accurate geographic setting and historical context of "A Resumed Identity," Bierce achieves several things. The story can be read as a tribute to his old brigade, recognizing it for its courage at Stone's River; it can be read simply as a bizarre psychological tale with a characteristic Biercean twist at the end; or it can be read autobiographically as a comment on Bierce coming to grips with his own mortality. Regardless, the detailed and accurate depiction of Hazen's Monument, that man-made terrain feature at the center of the story, gives a strong sense of verisimilitude to the extraordinary events of "A Resumed Identity."

Hazen's Brigade camped at Readyville, a small village about ten miles east of Murfreesboro, from January until June of 1863. Despite cavalry skirmishes, "constant vigilance, drilling and lessons," Hazen recalls this period of service as "a continued picnic. The season and climate were perfection." He adds, "good fortune never again brought to us such service" (*Narrative* 98). This general picture of relative safety helps explain how Hazen's men had time to build a monument. Hazen goes on to observe that at Readyville, "The isolation and proximity to the Rebel right, demanded the utmost vigilance; while the four companies of cavalry, given me for patrolling, during a large part of the time skirmished with the enemy nearly every day" (95). This scenario was to provide the setting for another Bierce supernatural tale.

"A Baffled Ambuscade" (1906) tells the story of a failed Confederate ambush along the Readyville and Woodbury Turnpike. Trooper Dunning, a Federal cavalryman, rides forward of his unit. A short time later shots ring out. Dunning's commander, Major Seidel, and his party ride along the dark road toward the noise. Major Seidel sees a dead horse and soldier on the road. Standing beside the bodies is Dunning, who silently motions the party to go back. About one hour later, after daybreak, the party rides forward again. The corpse in the road is actually that of Dunning, described as "hours dead" (III: 360). Seidel and party then find evidence that a strong force of Confederates vacated ambush positions near the body only about a half-hour before, their plan apparently thwarted by the appearance of Dunning's ghost.

"A Baffled Ambuscade" is the first of Bierce's war stories in which the entire action clearly takes place after Bierce became a topographer. The first paragraph of the piece sets it in historical and geographic context:

> Connecting Readyville and Woodbury was a good, hard turnpike nine or ten miles long. Readyville was an outpost of the Federal army at Murfreesboro; Woodbury had the same relation to the Confederate army at Tullahoma. For months after the big battle at Stone River these outposts were in constant quarrel, most of the trouble occurring, as one might expect, on the turnpike mentioned, between detachments of cavalry. (III: 356)

The historical accuracy of Bierce's description is not only borne out by Hazen's book but by the *Annals of the Army of the Cumberland* as well, which explains:

> Colonel Hazen's brigade was selected to hold the town of Readyville. [. . .] The enemy were constantly annoyed by expeditions against them. [. . .] On the 2d of April an expedition in command of General Hazen surprised a rebel camp at Woodbury, killing three and capturing about twenty-five men and horses. (John Fitch 223–24)

Hazen's *Narrative* describes the expedition and provides a detailed map of the pike with the plan of attack on Woodbury (map 6). Unfortunately the sketch map is unsigned and the identity of the cartographer cannot be determined; however, it is possible that the new brigade topographic engineer had a hand in it.

In describing the "ambuscade" executed on April 2, 1863, Hazen notes in his *Narrative*, "I have to speak in the highest terms of the battalion of the Third Ohio Cavalry, commanded by Major Seidel" (98). In "A Baffled Ambuscade," Bierce writes, "One night a squadron of Federal horse commanded by Major Seidel, a gallant and skillful officer, moved out of Readyville on an uncommonly hazardous enterprise requiring secrecy, caution and silence" (III: 356). Not only did Union

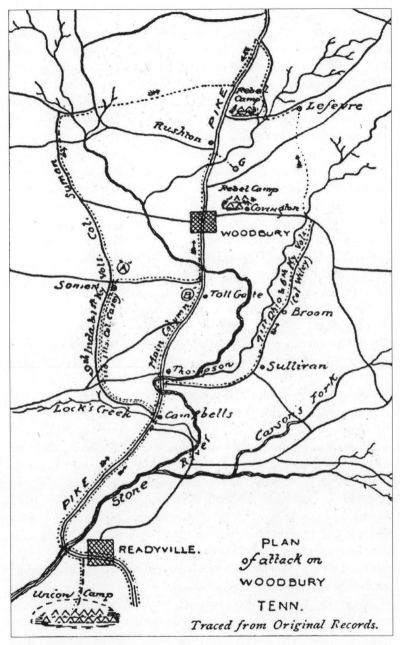

Map 6. Sketch map of Readyville to Woodbury Turnpike. This map may be a very early example of Bierce's work. From Hazen, *A Narrative of Military Service* (1885; Huntington, WV: Blue Acorn, 1993), facing p. 97.

and Confederate ambushes along the pike provide a general scenario for the story, Bierce uses Major Seidel by name as a character. Both Hazen and Bierce appear to admire Major Seidel, Hazen giving him accolades in *A Narrative of Military Service* and Bierce paying him tribute in "A Baffled Ambuscade."

Like the reference to General Hazen by name in "A Resumed Identity," Bierce's by-name use of someone he knew as a character, along with geographic and historical accuracy, adds plausibility to "A Baffled Ambuscade." These two supernatural stories reveal another important variation of Bierce's habitual craft techniques. Specifically, when Bierce tells a ghost or supernatural story, he tends to set it in a very specific location. The details of the setting are very true-to-life, and there are no significant modifications to extant features. Even today, Hazen's monument and its immediate vicinity are as described in "A Resumed Identity." Although the roads are asphalt now and there are more of them, even the sketch map (map 6) is accurate enough to permit one to trace the route of Trooper Dunning's adventure with relative ease. It now becomes apparent why Bierce did not write any ghost stories set in West Virginia. The nature of his duties there did not lend themselves to the recollection of terrain features with the degree of specificity evident in these mid-war tales out of Tennessee.

Bierce's tale "The Story of a Conscience" (1890) is of particular interest in that it provides a bridge of sorts between his stories of West Virginia and his stories of Tennessee. Like "Owl Creek Bridge," it reflects an interest in spies and saboteurs that comes to the fore here and in another tale, "Parker Adderson: Philosopher." "The Story of a Conscience" has two significant settings. The action of the story occurs in "an important defile in the Cumberland Mountains in Tennessee"; however, there is a significant flashback to Grafton, West Virginia (II: 167). As with this geographic nexus between two locations, the story is also a thematic bridge in that it connects the earlier Bierce motif of the lone sentry and later themes of the responsibilities, ethics, and duties of officership. This is a story Bierce probably would not have written had he not experienced both of these for himself.

In this story, Captain Parrol Hartroy, commander of an isolated detachment of Union troops in a small mountain town in Tennessee, discovers Drammer Brune, a Confederate spy, attempting to enter his lines with a forged pass. The captain recognizes the spy, having met him two years before. At the time, Hartroy was a private and Brune was a Union soldier who had deserted, become a Confederate spy, and been captured. Hartroy was assigned to guard Brune but fell asleep. The unshackled Brune, knowing that Hartroy could be put to death for sleeping on duty, does not escape and even goes so far as to wake Hartroy up when the sergeant of the guard approaches. Brune eventually does escape and remains a spy until his recapture. Now Captain Hartroy's duty is to sentence the spy to death, a sentence that Brune both accepts and fully expects. Hartroy, however, is so torn by the fact that he owes his life to Brune, and indeed Brune's would probably not be in jeopardy now had Brune not been so magnanimous previously, that Hartroy properly makes what he sees as fitting funeral arrangements, turns over his command, and, duty-bound, shoots himself at the same time the firing squad executes Brune.

Here again, Bierce's personal presence and regard for historical accuracy show themselves. During the flashback to autumn 1861, Captain Hartroy explains that he recognizes Brune as formerly "a private in an Ohio regiment" who deserted and joined the Confederates but was captured in a skirmish and sentenced to death (II: 172). Former private Hartroy was put on guard over Brune in "a freight car standing on a side track of a railway" in Grafton, West Virginia (II: 173). There were indeed three Ohio regiments in West Virginia in the fall of 1861 that fought alongside Bierce's Ninth Indiana. Grafton was a location familiar to all; it was, and still is, the rail center for the area. Incoming Federal regiments typically arrived via train in Grafton and then marched through Phillipi into the Cheat Mountain area. Although not explicitly stated, there is a strong implication that Brune and Hartroy were in the same regiment in West Virginia. Hartroy knows that before Brune went over to the Confederacy he was "a brave and trusted soldier" and that his defection was to "the surprise and grief of [. . . his] officers and comrades" (II: 172–73). The Twenty-fourth Ohio Volunteers, one of the three Ohio regiments in West Virginia in the autumn of 1861, later became a part of Hazen's Brigade and was posted in various locations in the Cumberland Mountains in Tennessee during the summer and early fall of 1863. Even in this brief flashback, Bierce is perfectly historically accurate.

Moreover, even this spy story has some ties to one that involved the Ninth Indiana Volunteers while the unit was in West Virginia. In early September 1861, while the Ninth was back in Indiana and mustering again for three years' service and redeployment to West Virginia, several members of the unit recognized a suspicious civilian they remembered from Phillipi, less than fifteen miles from Grafton. Officers from the regiment arrested the man, whose name was John C. Brain, and discovered on him papers identifying him as a member of a "disloyal secret organization known as the Knights of the Golden Circle" and as a member of a unit of the Confederate Kentucky State Guard (*OR* 2/II: 711). Brain claimed he was a daguerreotypist, but evidence quickly mounted indicating he was recruiting volunteers for the Confederacy, sketching railroad facilities, and smuggling pistols and ammunition to the South. Secretary of State William Seward ordered Brain imprisoned in New York within a few days of his arrest. Brain, however, appealed to the British ambassador, claiming that he was born in London and was still a citizen of England. After several exchanges of correspondence between Seward and the ambassador, Brain was released in February 1862 after he took an oath stipulating that he would not return to any southern states, would have no correspondence with anyone in those states without Seward's permission, and would not "do anything hostile to the United States during the present insurrection" (*OR* 2/II: 718). Bierce would have been familiar with this story, and the fact that the name Brain so closely resembles Brune makes it all the more likely that it was part of the inspiration for "The Story of a Conscience."

Captain Hartroy's position in "an important defile in the Cumberland Mountains in Tennessee" might seem impossibly vague and, although an actual counterpart cannot be positively identified from the information given, one can narrow the possibilities significantly. Although most associate the Cumberland Mountains with the site of the famous Cumberland Gap on the Kentucky-Virginia-Tennessee border, the Cumberlands extend the entire length of mideastern Tennessee (map 7). Hazen's Brigade became quite familiar with the Tennessee Cumberlands. During the time the brigade was in the Readyville-Woodbury area, it was near the western edge of the Cumberland Escarpment. During July, August, and early September 1863, as part of the Tullahoma Campaign and the move on Chattanooga that culminated in the battle at Chickamauga, Hazen's Brigade was in the Cumberlands. The brigade first encamped near Manchester on the western side of the mountains, then moved across the Cumberland Plateau to Poe's Tavern (now just south of the twin towns of Soddy and Daisy) on the eastern side just north of Chattanooga. Hazen commanded a large force, detached from the rest of the Army of the Cumberland, with the mission of guarding the western side of the Tennessee River and making the Confederates think that the bulk of the Union forces were along the river north of Chattanooga, when in reality they had swung south and intended to cross the river at Bridgeport, Tennessee (Hazen 103).

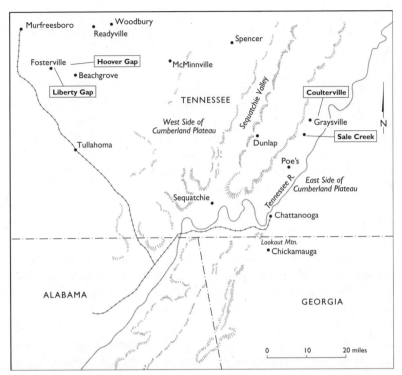

Map 7. The Cumberland Plateau region.

The topography of the Cumberlands in this part of Tennessee is fairly simple: the mountains rise sharply and form western and eastern escarpments as borders; between them is a relatively flat plateau sharply cut at its southern end by the Sequatchie River valley. The Sequatchie Valley divides the plateau along a roughly north–south axis and adds two more lengthy escarpments down the center of the plateau. The eastern side of the plateau is Walden Ridge, which runs northeast out of Chattanooga and parallels the Sequatchie and Tennessee Rivers (map 7). Militarily, to control the gaps or passes along the roads that lead up onto the plateau is to control the plateau. Once a force is on the plateau, movement is relatively easy. In his memoir, Hazen notes:

> We picketed the [Tennessee] river and watched every possible point of crossing for fifty miles [. . .]. The Tennessee valley [. . .] being shut in by the almost vertical face of Waldon's [*sic*] Ridge, with but few practicable ascents, which we soon found and thoroughly understood, and as they

       1863, Stone's River to Chickamauga and Missionary Ridge

were easily defensible, our position was excellent; for if hard pressed, we had only to take possession of the ridge and defend these few passes. (*Narrative* 103–4)

On September 6, 1863, Hazen told Colonel Minty, one of his cavalry commanders, "The several roads leading from Pikeville to McMinnville can probably be obstructed at the mountain, so as to cause a delay of a day or so, or a detour toward Sparta [. . .] be prepared to obstruct in advance of your arrival in the Sequatchie" (*Narrative* 109–10). The important point here is that Hazen's troops were, for a time, relatively far-flung, watching both the critical mountain passes and possible crossing points along the Tennessee River. No doubt Ambrose Bierce was involved in scouting and mapping the "practicable ascents" and "several roads" that lead across the Cumberland Plateau.

Hazen's *Narrative* further demonstrates Bierce's faithfulness to the context of the Tullahoma campaign. Hazen records that during this time in the Cumberlands his units "gathered a great quantity of forage and food, and were hospitably entertained by a rather primitive and strongly Union people. In my command, systematic foraging was here introduced" (103). In "The Story of a Conscience" Bierce writes: "To a few resident civilians of known loyalty, with whom it was desirable to trade, and of whose services in various ways [Hartroy] sometimes availed himself, he had given written passes admitting them within his lines" (II: 168). This statement rings true with the situation Hazen describes.

The town of Spencer, in Van Buren County, Tennessee, is an excellent example of the type of "important defile in the Cumberland Mountains in Tennessee" that Bierce had in mind when he wrote "The Story of a Conscience." Spencer is on the western side of the Cumberland Plateau; east and slightly north of McMinnville, the town sits at the top of the escarpment and is on the site of one of the few roads, even today, between Pikeville and McMinnville. The east–west road through Spencer, apparent on Civil War maps, is now Tennessee Highway 30 and winds through a series of defiles or gaps to both the east and west of the town. Union troops occupied the town in 1863 and 1864. One fairly detailed county history tells of "a squadron of cavalry and a wagon train" that camped at Spencer in the winter of 1864 and "collected supplies from the surrounding country" (Medley 164). The same history also notes that "guerilla forces combed the countryside" during those years. The situation in Spencer resonates remarkably with the setting Bierce creates in "The Story of a Conscience." Hartroy's detachment, at considerable "distance from the main army" and guarding "an important defile" that "was on a turnpike" (II: 168,167, 165) might well have been part of a brigade like Hazen's, widely dispersed through the Cumberland Mountains to secure the many mountain passes and river crossing sites. Guerrilla activity was common in Van Buren County; Hartroy must concern himself with the "lawless character of the enemy's irregular troops infesting that region" (II: 168). Spencer was occupied by a cavalry squadron "and a wagon train"; Hartroy has "a company of infantry, a squadron of cavalry, and a section of artillery" (II: 167). While it is impossible to say with certainty that Spencer is the small town in the important defile that Bierce had in mind, it certainly serves as an excellent example of just how faithful Bierce was to the terrain and the tactical situation prevalent in the Tennessee Cumberlands during the late summer of 1863.

This story is a revealing combination of themes. In the flashback to Grafton, Bierce reverts to his most common West Virginia motif, the lone guard or sentinel. This time, however, there is a bit of a twist in that it is the prisoner, not the guard, who must make the first moral decision. That is to say, it is Drammer Brune who makes the decision not to escape from (and thus spares the life of) the sleeping Private Hartroy. It is not until two or three years later that Hartroy must make his own moral decision, a decision that, in effect, evens the score from their earlier encounter. What makes a critical difference to Hartroy is the fact that he is now an officer—something he, like Bierce, was not when he was in West Virginia. The duties and responsibilities of officership suddenly move to the center of the story. The demands of what he sees as his duty are, in fact, what sends Hartroy to his own death.

In "The Story of a Conscience," Hartroy's original offense of sleeping on duty could have earned him a death penalty. As it was, his action had no immediate consequence thanks to Brune's decision not to escape. Two years later, as an officer and commander of a very isolated post who had "wisely been given corresponding discretionary powers," including the power to order summary executions, Captain Hartroy must confront the military crime he committed as Private Hartroy (II: 168). Now he has both the authority and, he feels, the duty to execute not just enemy spies but, even long after the fact, sleeping sentinels as well.

Tellingly and by now predictably, Bierce sets the action of this story in Tennessee in what is probably 1863. To have cast essentially the same events in 1861 or 1862 would have been very uncharacteristic. Bierce needed to experience, to some degree, both of the situations that Hartroy finds himself in. That is to say, Bierce needed to have been both the private on sentry duty and the officer responsible for the privates on sentry duty before he could write a story that incorporates both in one character. As the issues in his stories become more complicated, one should note that Bierce does not abandon earlier themes. The lone sentry of West Virginia, for example, is present in "The Story of a Conscience"; however, now the intricacies of military rank and the demands of officership are added to the mix. Here then is an excellent example of Bierce's work reflecting his professional growth as a soldier.

The higher up in the army he moved, the more intricate were the situations that Bierce encountered. Hazen was certainly a commander concerned with the business of officership. During the relative lull following the battle at Stone's River, Hazen reestablished the rigorous sorts of training regimens and schools for soldiers for which he was noted. He did not simply direct endless drilling for his enlisted soldiers. A dispatch from Hazen in early March, the month Bierce joined the staff, reflects some of Hazen's concerns for the professional development of his officers:

> [Officers of] [t]he entire brigade, including staff and headquarters [are] to be instructed [. . .]. Theoretical instruction will commence immediately, with Hardee's "Tactics." All commissioned officers are to recite daily from 10 to 11.30 A.M. A complete report of recitations will be submitted daily. Practical instruction will also begin immediately. [. . .] The Forty-first Ohio Volunteers will be carried through the course already prescribed as rapidly as possible; then beginning with Jomini's "Art of War," and reading in Napier's "Peninsular War." The officers of this regiment are informed that it is expected that they will keep up the course of study and reading that they have entered upon, as long as they remain in the service.
>
> The foregoing school is in view of an examination by a board of officers, before which it is proposed to bring every officer of the command. (*Narrative* 95–96)

It comes as no surprise, then, that understudying a man Bierce characterized as "my commander and my friend, my master in the art of war" for whom "duty was his religion" produced similar concerns about what it means to be an officer—concerns that are prevalent in war stories such as "The Story of a Conscience," "The Affair at Coulter's Notch," "Jupiter Doke," "One Kind of Officer," "Two Military Executions," and "Killed at Resaca" (I: 284).

Another story of spies in which the executioner ironically ends up dying along with the executed is "Parker Adderson, Philosopher."[3] The unique feature of this story is that it is the only one that Bierce tells from the Confederate side of the lines. The action takes place wholly in a Confederate encampment in and around the commanding officer's tent. Parker Adderson is a Union sergeant and a spy who, having been captured in the evening, expects to be hanged the following morning. Adderson gives a series of flippant answers to the commander's questions and makes light of his impending doom. The commander orders that Adderson be shot by a firing squad immediately; this unexpected sentence so totally unnerves the prisoner that he starts fighting with his captors and pulls down the tent on top of everyone. In the ensuing confusion, the commander is seriously wounded and shortly thereafter peacefully dies at the same time the firing squad executes Adderson.

While the wisecracking Union spy is arguably the protagonist, certainly the southern commander, General Clavering, plays an equally vital role. In fact, despite the title of the story, one might consider the general as the central character. After all, the opening and closing lines of dialogue belong to Clavering, nicely framing the tale. The story is, in fact, as Cathy Davidson and Mary Grenander have pointed out, a role reversal of sorts (Davidson, *Experimental* 68–69, Grenander 84). Clavering, who initially insists, "Death is horrible!" goes very serenely into that good night, while flippant and scoffing Adderson becomes something of a gibbering idiot when faced with his imminent and unexpected demise (II: 139).

The reason the title identifies Adderson as a philosopher is most likely that he attempts to present several of the same points about death as Socrates does in his famous defense that Plato recorded in the "Apology." Yet, like his dying, Adderson does it very badly. For example, Socrates claims:

> To fear death, gentlemen, is no other than to think oneself wise when one is not, to think one knows what one does not. No one knows whether death may not be the greatest of all blessings for a man, yet men fear it as if they knew that it is the greatest of evils. And sure it is the most blameworthy ignorance to believe that one knows what one does not know. [. . .] I shall never fear or avoid things of which I do not know. (29 a, b)

Adderson, responding to Clavering's question, "Do you know that this is a serious matter?" replies:

> How can I know that? I have never been dead in all my life. I have heard that death is a serious matter, but never from any of those who have experienced it. [. . .] A loss of [any present happiness and future opportunities] which we shall never be conscious can be borne with composure

and therefore expected without apprehension. You must have observed, General, that of all the dead men with whom it is your soldierly pleasure to strew your path none shows signs of regret. (II: 137)

Not only Adderson's words, but his actions as well become pale imitations of the classical philosophical exemplar. Presented with the chance to escape easily, Socrates refused, insisting instead on standing for his principles to the end. Adderson, however, makes a desperate and almost ridiculously futile escape attempt; his actions stand in stark contrast to his own blithely expressed philosophy.

The character names in this story also carry ironic significance. The verb *claver* is of Scottish origin and means to prate or gossip. General clavering is certainly something the character of the same name is not guilty of; however, his prisoner does it throughout most of the tale. The prisoner's name poses an interesting problem. Adderson, with its suggestion of the offspring of a snake, seems a particularly appropriate name for him. Although the European variety is venomous, American adders are nonpoisonous despite popular misconceptions (especially in the nineteenth century). Because Bierce lived in England for three years, he probably had the venomous version in mind when he titled the story as well as when he wrote the following entry for *The Devil's Dictionary*: "ADDER, *n*. A species of snake. So called from its habit of adding funeral outlays to the expenses of living" (VII: 19). Parker Adderson, after all, is not only the claverer of the story, but his encounter with the general, despite his seemingly ineffectual or nonpoisonous words, proves a fatal bite to both men.

But the questions still remain why Bierce would tell this one story from the Confederate point of view and how it relates to Bierce's soldierly development. Perhaps some of the influence is due to Bierce's own brief capture. The only apparent parallel to the story of Parker Adderson is that Bierce, as mentioned earlier, expressed some concern that he might be hanged should the local guerrilla chief learn of his capture. His captors, however, actually protected him from such a fate as they attempted to evacuate him to military headquarters. Nonetheless, the fact is that the only story Bierce tells from a Confederate perspective is about a Union prisoner of war who might be hanged, something he once was himself.

This interest in spies can further be explained, at least in part, by another, more celebrated spy case than that of John C. Brain, one that became familiar to the soldiers of Hazen's Brigade in 1863. The story of

Sam Davis is a possible analogue for the stories of both Peyton Farquhar and Parker Adderson. Davis was a twenty-one-year-old soldier in the Confederate army who was a member of a group of scouts dispatched by General Braxton Bragg to work behind Union lines and report troop movements to the Confederate forces laying siege to Chattanooga. In November 1863, Union forces captured Davis at Pulaski, Tennessee, along the Tennessee and Alabama railroad line and only twenty-four miles north of the Sulphur Creek Trestle in northern Alabama. Davis had on his person details of Union plans and activities throughout middle Tennessee.

Subsequent events read like something out of a Bierce story. General Greenville Dodge, the man who would go on to build the Union Pacific Railroad, was the Federal commander at Pulaski and suspected that someone in his own command might have passed documents to Davis. Davis, however, refused to disclose any information about his mission. Dodge later wrote, "I pleaded with him and urged him with all the power I possessed to give me some chance to save his life, for I had discovered he was a most admirable young fellow" (qtd. in Brandt 268). Although Davis was in a Confederate uniform, his location deep behind enemy lines caused Dodge to pronounce a spy's sentence—hanging the next morning, the one Parker Adderson expected. Davis rode in a wagon sitting atop his own coffin to the gallows. General Dodge tried one last time to offer Davis his life in return for the informant's name. Davis, in true Nathan Hale–like (and decidedly not Parker Adderson–like) fashion stated, "No, I cannot. I had rather die a thousand deaths than betray a friend, or be false to duty" (qtd. in Brandt 269). Thus the young Confederate went to his death espousing the ideals of courage, loyalty, and duty reflected in many a Bierce protagonist but without the corresponding complication of a broken rope, a broken duty, or a broken psyche. Sam Davis became a local hero and martyr. A statue of him stands in front of the county courthouse in Pulaski, in addition to a Davis shrine on Davis Street. Davis's home in Smyrna is a state historic site. Considering all the local notoriety that the Davis case received, it is unsurprising that Bierce casts the action of his two spy stories in 1863.

Although the story of bungling saboteur Peyton Farquhar's hanging has largely kept Bierce's work in the public eye, ultimately his treatment of spies is of relatively minor importance in his war stories. Read in isolation, both "Parker Adderson" and "The Story of a Conscience" are reasonably good stories. Read in the context of other Bierce war tales, most readers will quickly predict that both the spies and their captors will die in the end. Thus the appearance of saboteurs and spies is largely a plot device or scenario that provides the author with an opportunity to explore the larger themes of duty, death, one's duty to die honorably, and especially in the case of "The Story of a Conscience," the entailments of officership.

By now, one probably has begun to notice some patterns in Bierce's character-naming practices. A study of no small scale would be necessary to investigate character names in his war stories adequately, and it will be discussed only briefly here. At times he enjoys a bit of punning and word play, as with Bennett Greene in "Two Military Executions" and General Clavering and his prisoner in "Parker Adderson, Philosopher." At other times he commemorates someone he admires by inserting his name in the tale as with General Hazen in "A Resumed Identity" or Major Seidel in "A Baffled Ambuscade." At still other times Bierce uses names that he apparently heard along the way. The mustering officer for the Ninth Indiana Volunteers, for example, had the same surname as the protagonist of "An Occurrence at Owl Creek Bridge."

A similar use of surnames occurs in "The Affair at Coulter's Notch" (1889). The story is set on a pleasant summer afternoon in the South. A turnpike runs through a narrow pass, or notch, one so slim that only a single cannon at a time can be in firing position beside the road. Half a mile away, on the enemy's side of the notch, is a plantation house with two Confederate artillery batteries in the yard. A Union general orders one of his brigade commanders to have his artillery engage the Confederate guns. Captain Coulter, whom the general seems to disdain, commands the brigade's artillery battery. The brigade commander, a colonel with a high opinion of Coulter, points out to no avail that it would be one gun against twelve. After being given the order, Coulter briefly questions the necessity of it and receives only a stony look from the general who turns and rides off. Coulter's seeming reluctance to obey orders deeply embarrasses the colonel, but before he can speak, Coulter gives the order to his battery. When the artillery duel begins, the Federal gunners concentrate most of their fire on a Confederate cannon visible on the lawn of the plantation house. Many of the shells strike the house. A nearby infantry regimental commander reports that the Confederate gun crews are within range of his rifles, but the general has ordered the infantry to hold its fire. As they watch the battle from a distance, the brigade commander and his adjutant converse. The young adjutant asks the colonel if he knows that Coulter is from the South. The commander does not. The adjutant then repeats a story he is certain is true. According to the adjutant, the division that the general had commanded the previous summer was once camped near the Coulter home. The general became acquainted with Coulter's wife and family. Then, the adjutant explains:

> There was trouble—I don't know the exact nature of it—something about Coulter's wife. She is a red-hot Secessionist, as they all are, except Coulter himself, but she is a good wife and high-bred lady. There was a complaint to army headquarters. The general was transferred to this division. It is odd that Coulter's battery should afterward have been assigned to it. (III: 114)

The colonel suddenly realizes why the general ordered such an obviously tactically unsound operation. As several critics have noted, the appearance of the word *affair* in the title is a rather heavy-handed clue.[4] Having heard Coulter's gun silent for a few minutes, then a new one resume firing, the colonel rides over to tell Coulter to withdraw the piece. The colonel finds the gun position to be a hellhole. Not one but four of Coulter's guns have been destroyed, and much of his battery lies dead or wounded. The artillerymen had been replacing the single firing gun so quickly that there was never a lull in the bombardment until many of them were killed or wounded. Even the cannon appears to be bleeding, having been swabbed with a rammer accidentally dipped in a pool of blood. Coulter, like his soldiers, is bloody and blackened with soot and grime. The colonel orders the barrage halted and the gun withdrawn. A short time later the Union troops occupy the Confederate's former positions. The colonel makes his headquarters in the badly damaged plantation house. During dinner that evening, an orderly reports to the colonel that something is wrong in the basement of the house. The two go into the dim basement and discover a gruesome tableau: in a corner is a man holding the dead bodies of a woman and child. The woman still clutches the infant in her arms. Shortly, the man looks up at the two soldiers. The colonel asks the man what he is doing there and the man replies that the house belongs to him. "And these?" asks the colonel, referring to the corpses. The man replies, "My wife and child. I am Captain Coulter" (III: 121).

After such an intense conclusion, it is as a bit of a relief to know that Coulter's Notch is an invented place. However, the fictional notch is not without factual prototypes. The story itself affords few specific clues as to its location. It is summertime in southern territory; the adjutant's remarks indicate that Union troops had been in the area around Coulter's home the previous summer. Tennessee immediately seems a likely location for the action. The Union army first moved into middle and eastern Tennessee in very early 1862 and campaigned there throughout 1862 and 1863. If "The Affair at Coulter's Notch" occurs a year after the army had first been in the area, then it would be the summer of 1863 or 1864. The summer of 1864 is unlikely because the Union army was by that time pushing through northwestern Georgia toward Atlanta.

In late June of 1863, General Rosecrans ordered the Army of the Cumberland to begin advancing in force over the road networks in middle Tennessee, his objective being to take control of Tullahoma, where, as Bierce mentions in "A Baffled Ambuscade," the bulk of the Confederate Army of Tennessee was encamped. Rosecrans's final objective was the capture of Chattanooga in extreme southeastern Tennessee. His plan was a brilliant combination of feints and flanking movements that avoided frontal attacks on Confederate strong points located in four mountain passes or gaps along the roads (a notch is a small gap). These gaps were only about ten miles out of Murfreesboro and, as recorded in the *Annals of the Army of the Cumberland*, they "were the key of the position, and their loss to the enemy at once determined him to retreat" (John Fitch 223–24). While advancing, Rosecrans's troops fought significant actions in both Liberty Gap and Hoover Gap on June 24,1863, with the battle at Liberty Gap concluding on June 25. In describing the action on the second day at Liberty Gap, John Fitch explains, "Placing the Louisville Legion (5th Kentucky) on the right and the 6th Indiana on the left of the road [. . .] and directing a section of the 5th Ohio Battery, under Lieutenant Ellison, to engage the rebel artillery [battery], [Colonel Baldwin] moved to the attack" (445). An artillery section is two guns; a Civil War battery had from four to eight. Here was a tactical scenario with some resemblance to the one at Coulter's Notch: specifically, outgunned Federal artillery with infantry on both sides of the road along a ridge line. Topographically, both Hoover Gap and Liberty Gap also resemble the terrain Bierce creates at Coulter's Notch: a road through a narrow pass, civilian houses on the Confederate side, and a stream near the houses. Of the two, the terrain at Liberty Gap is a much closer match to the road that makes "a sinuous ascent through a thin forest" and "a similar, though less steep, descent" described in the story (II: 105). Confederate General John R. Liddell, in his official report, noted that Union artillery firing from Liberty Gap "struck the chimney of a Mr. Jones' house" (Scott and Lazelle 588). No mention is made in the official reports of any civilian casualties; however, Liddell's account and the map that accompanies it confirm damage to at least one dwelling in the area.

Although nearby, Hazen's Brigade was not involved in the action in the gaps. His troops did not move out of Readyville until June 26. After their six-month "picnic," Hazen's men marched down the pikes to Manchester as part of Rosecrans's effort to outflank the Rebels at Tullahoma. After one month at Manchester, Hazen's Brigade continued its march towards Chattanooga, passing through the Cumberland Mountains as described earlier. The brigade's route had taken them through many gaps, passes, and notches along the Tennessee roads.

By August 22, 1863, Hazen had made Poe's Tavern his headquarters, where he would remain until September 9 or 10. Poe's Tavern was little more than a country crossroads, but it served as the first courthouse of Hamilton County from the establishment of the county in 1820 until the county seat was moved to Chattanooga (map 7). One of the 765 original white settlers of Hamilton County was Thomas Coulter, who died in 1876 and is buried in a church graveyard near Sale Creek, just north of Poe's (Armstrong 261). Coulter became a common name in the county through the 1800s.

Giving some sense of the divided loyalties in the area and just how faithful Bierce is to history, there were two Coulters from Tennessee who enlisted in Tennessee regiments that fought for the Union and twenty-four who enlisted in Tennessee regiments that fought for the Confederacy (Tennessee Civil War Centennial Commission 106, 495). In August 1863, while Hazen's Brigade was at Poe's Tavern, James J. Coulter from Hamilton County enlisted in the Union army and, like the fictional Captain Coulter, served in an Ohio artillery battery until the end of the war (Sistler and Sistler 70).

General Hazen was quite impressed by how loyal the citizens north of Chattanooga were to the Union. In his memoir he claims, "The people are more loyal than many of those of Ohio and Indiana, and often the corn and hay belongs to women whose husbands are in our army" (*Narrative* 106). Although Mrs. Coulter may not have been strongly Union, the second part of Hazen's statement is certainly evocative of Bierce's story. Hazen was also familiar with the Sale Creek area where Thomas Coulter lived. On September 8, he sent one of his regiments across the Tennessee River at the mouth of the creek (*Narrative* 119). Even today, the community that lies along Sale Creek, less than ten miles north of Poe's Tavern, is called "Coulterville" and is situated at the bottom of the eastern face of the Cumberland Escarpment, an area with many mountain gaps or notches.

There is no doubt that Hazen and Bierce encountered the name "Coulter" during their stay at Poe's. James J. Coulter's enlistment in an Ohio artillery unit presents the intriguing possibility that Bierce may have drawn on some personal knowledge of Coulter's situation as a source for "The Affair at Coulter's Notch." The evidence, though purely circumstantial, is remarkable. The Army of the Cumberland was involved in at least two fairly well-documented engagements in middle Tennessee in the summer of 1863 with terrain and tactical scenarios that resemble those of "The Affair at Coulter's Notch." At least one of those resulted in damage to a civilian home. A short time later, Hazen's Brigade marched through the ridge-filled terrain to a place where Coulter is a common name. While Hazen was there, a southerner named James Coulter enlisted in a Union artillery battery. It seems too long a string of extraordinary coincidences for Bierce not to have incorporated some of them in formulating his war story.

The terrain is an essential element of "The Affair at Coulter's Notch." Bierce needed a very narrow gap with a road through it and a civilian home on the enemy side of the gap. There were many such places in middle Tennessee, but none with historic circumstances quite as remarkable as those associated with the story. Here again, as in "A Horseman in the Sky," to tell such a powerful story in a setting that actually exists would be to risk losing credibility, as a reader familiar with the place might know that, in fact, such an affair never really happened there. Like the bridge at Owl Creek, Coulter's Notch is fictional terrain that is a composite of actual elements and serves as a setting for a story drawn from Bierce's experiences in the summer of 1863.

Like Bierce's other 1863 stories, the duties and responsibilities of being an officer are at the fore of "The Affair at Coulter's Notch." Although the protagonist here must, like those in the West Virginia stories, make a moral decision that involves the gravest of consequences, no longer is that protagonist physically isolated. Coulter's position as an artillery battery commander puts him in a very public light, subject to the intense scrutiny of both the men under him and the chain of command over him. This makes Coulter's decision to comply with the order all the more complex. Coulter's compliance threatens not only members of his family but the soldiers he commands as well. To put his battery, one gun at a time, into a position subject to the fire of twelve Confederate pieces is putting his men in unnecessarily grave danger. The general clearly comprehends the predicament he is placing Coulter in. To comply with the order puts Coulter, his family, and his soldiers at risk; to refuse it would probably mean a court-martial for Coulter and disgrace for his battery. Even the colonel knows from the outset that something is very wrong, but he initially complies with the order because the "spirit of military subordination is not favorable to retort, nor even to deprecation" (II: 107). Unlike the decision the lone sentinel of "A Horseman in the Sky" must make, Coulter's involves corporate action and responsibility. It is the sort of command responsibility that belongs only with an officer and not with an isolated sentry.

Duty, officership, and artillerymen move to the thematic center once again in "One Kind of Officer" (1893), a story that has drawn virtually no critical attention and that seems an obvious pairing with "Coulter's Notch." It would be easy to classify this story as one in which Bierce seems to exhaust the possibilities of soldiers killing themselves, family, or fellows—all the while complicating the issue of just who the enemy is. Captain Hartroy and several other protagonists commit suicide; Carter Druse kills his father; William Grayrock shoots his brother; Captain Coulter kills his wife and child; in "One Kind of Officer," Captain Ransome, the protagonist, kills other Union soldiers. The story is, however, even more complex than that. It is another of Bierce's examinations of leadership and is a story that demonstrates those qualities that a good officer ought not to have. Captain Ransome, unlike Captain Coulter, Carter Druse, and Captain Parrol Hartroy, does not face a moral dilemma. His problem is a sense of wounded pride and an overarching arrogance concerning his own scheme for revenge, a retribution gone horribly wrong.

"One Kind of Officer" examines two officers: one a general and the other a captain who commands an artillery battery. General Cameron, a brigade commander, does not have a high opinion of Captain Ransome, the battery commander, and as the story opens, the general is dressing down the captain: "Captain Ransome, it is not permitted to you to know *anything*. It is sufficient that you obey my order—which permit me to repeat. If you perceive any movement of troops in your front you are to open fire, and if attacked hold this position as long as you can" (II: 178). The only witness to the conversation is Ransome's lieutenant. In the rain and heavy fog of the day, two of Ransome's soldiers report hearing movements and voices to their front that they believe to be the enemy. Ransome listens to the report and orders his lieutenant to have the battery open fire with grapeshot. A heated battle ensues in the fog; infantry charges against Ransome's positions and is repulsed. Ransome's lieutenant emotionally reports something to Ransome, but the reader is privy only to Ransome's reply: "Lieutenant Price, it is not permitted to you to know *anything*. It is sufficient that you obey my orders" (II: 191). The infantry retreats and the guns fall silent. It quickly becomes obvious that the enemy was, in reality, another Union regiment attempting to move into position on Ransome's flank in the heavy fog. It is possible Ransome knew this from the start, and his conversation with the animated Lieutenant Price certainly confirms the identity of the unit to their front. Ransome sought to avenge the general's earlier insult by carrying out his orders to the letter. The division commander arrives on the scene and, naturally quite agitated by the carnage, demands to know why Ransome knowingly fired into another Union regiment. Ransome, thinking he will deflect all blame to General Cameron, refers the division commander to him. But Cameron has died in the fight, and Lieutenant Price, the only witness to the original order, having been insulted by Ransome in the same manner as Cameron insulted him, denies any knowledge of the orders under which Ransome was operating. Ransome realizes his scheme has failed. Somewhat like "Owl Creek Bridge," this tale ends with a flash-forward by the protagonist to his own death by firing squad. Ransome imagines postmortem sensations. Whereas Peyton Farquhar imagines his escape from death, Captain Ransome hears "the sound of the earth upon his coffin" and "the song of a bird above his forgotten grave" a few seconds after realizing the enormity of his actions and long before he is dead (II: 196). Ransome, knowing that he is now doomed, hands over his saber to the provost marshal.

There are no topographical clues in the story as to its location. Ransome's battery is on the extreme northern (left) flank of an army that faces generally eastward. The Army of the Cumberland's movement during the Tullahoma campaign was generally to the east and south. That fact, however, is far too little to claim that the action is in Tennessee. Tactically, his position atop a hill is an excellent one for his guns. However, there are no significant indications of where or when the action of the story occurs. What is described in some detail is the weather: cold, rainy, and very foggy. Most remarkable is the fog. Unlike many Bierce stories, this one does not begin on a fair, sunny day that is only an ironic harbinger of the grim events soon to unfold. This time the story begins in a thick and ever-present fog that sets an eerie, macabre tone much like that of *Macbeth* or portions of *Julius Caesar*. The fog occasionally opens briefly, only to close again, like stage curtains, as the protagonist heads toward his inevitable downfall. In a bit of foreshadowing, Captain Ransome stands alone at the end of the first chapter of the story, and the "gray fog, thickening every moment, closed in about him like a visible doom" (II: 179).

Despite its lack of distinctive terrain, however, juxtaposing "One Kind of Officer" with "The Affair at Coulter's Notch" provides an interesting series of contrasts. Both stories have protagonists who are artillery battery commanders; in both, the commanders at the next two levels figure prominently; in each story, one of the senior commanders thinks highly of the battery commander, while the other has a low opinion of him; and both stories revolve around obedience to orders and the killing of those other than the enemy. In many respects, it seems that Bierce was rehashing elements of "Coulter's Notch" when he wrote "One Kind of Officer." But there is a fundamental difference between Captain Ransome and most Bierce protagonists: Ransome is not a brave and capable soldier attempting to do the right thing only to discover the forces of battlefield fate are more capricious than he could imagine. Like many Bierce heroes, he is naïve, but his naïveté lies in believing that his vengeful scheme will succeed. Ransome commits one of the most egregious sins an officer can make—he overlooks the ideal of selfless service and uses his position in an attempt at personal gain, that is, to gain revenge against the officer who slighted him. When Ransome attempts to repeat General Cameron's bad example of officership with Lieutenant Price, his fate is as much sealed as the already dead general's. Unlike Coulter, who dutifully carries out an order that is dubious at best, Ransome arrogantly executes an order that he dutifully should have complied with in its spirit, but clearly not in its letter. Ransome, then, is perverting the concept of duty and officership held in such high regard by Bierce. That Bierce subscribed to such a view is borne out not only by his fiction but by a newspaper column from 1883 in which he stated that "the life of an army officer commonly is, and always is likely to be, one of exceptional labor, self-denial and responsibility" (*Wasp* 22 Dec. 1883). Although Ransome will, like many Bierce protagonists, die, his will not be an honorable death. He is the antithesis of the kind of officer that one should be.

The contrast between the two battery commanders during the thick of the fighting exemplifies their differences. The narrator describes a literally hellish scene as Coulter's battery duels with the Confederates. When the brigade commander rides over to the battery to find Coulter and tell him to cease firing,

> [a] fiend seven times damned sprang out of the smoke to take [a wounded soldier's] place, but paused and gazed up at the mounted officer with an unearthly regard, his teeth flashing between his black lips, his eyes, fierce and expanded, burning like coals beneath his bloody brow. The colonel made an authoritative gesture and pointed to the rear. The fiend bowed in token of obedience. It was Captain Coulter. (II: 117)

In contrast to Coulter, who is very much in the thick of the fighting, even to the point of helping man a gun himself, Ransome is imperiously aloof and isolated while his battery is in action and under an attack that is becoming hand-to-hand. The narrator explains:

> As the commander of a battery in action can find something better to do than cracking individual skulls, Captain Ransome had retired from the parapet to his proper post in rear of his guns, where he stood with folded arms, his bugler beside him. Here, during the hottest of the fight, he was approached by Lieutenant Price [. . .]. (II: 190)

These actions reflect their differing characters. Coulter can "find something better to do" by lending a badly needed hand; Ransome retreats to the traditional battery commander's spot rather than lending a hand in the increasingly close combat.

Along with its affinities to "Coulter's Notch," the aspect of this story that most strongly supports its placement as a story set in 1863 or possibly 1864 is its insight into a variety of levels of the army. This was the sort of knowledge that its author simply did not have until well into the third year of the war. In "One Kind of Officer" Bierce adeptly shifts the focus from conversations among higher-ranking officers to views of lower-ranking enlisted soldiers at work.

This story will never be a classic, but much of its value is simply in the vignettes of an army that it presents. In the opening scene of the story, for example, just after the initial confrontation between General Cameron and Captain Ransome, the narrator explains:

> For a moment General Cameron and the commander of the battery sat in their saddles, looking at each other in silence. There was no more to say; apparently too much had already been said. Then the superior officer nodded coldly and turned his horse to ride away. The artillerist saluted slowly, gravely, and with extreme formality. One acquainted with the niceties of military etiquette would have said that by his manner he attested a sense of the rebuke that he had incurred. It is one of the important uses of civility to signify resentment. (II: 178–79)

Equally insightful is a description of Ransome's battery at work:

> The gunners worked alertly, but without haste or apparent excitement. There was really no reason for excitement; it is not much to point a cannon into a fog and fire it. [. . .]
>
> The men smiled at their noisy work, performing it with a lessening alacrity. They cast curious regards upon their captain [. . .]. Suddenly out of the obscurity burst a great sound of cheering [. . .] the sound

was inexpressibly strange—so loud, so near, so menacing, yet nothing seen! The men who had smiled at their work smiled no more, but performed it with a serious and feverish activity. (II: 188–89)

Most insightful are the narrator's observations of the army as a whole:

An army has a personality. Beneath the individual thoughts and emotions of its component parts it thinks and feels as a unit. And in this large, inclusive sense of things lies a wiser wisdom than the mere sum of all that it knows. On that dismal morning this great brute force, groping at the bottom of a white ocean of fog among trees that seemed as sea weeds, had a dumb consciousness that all was not well; that a day's manœuvring had resulted in a faulty disposition of its parts, a blind diffusion of its strengths. (II: 181–82)

The narrator, with characteristic ability to quickly cut across levels of command, then continues:

The men felt insecure and talked among themselves of such tactical errors as with their meager military vocabulary they were able to name. Field and line officers gathered in groups and spoke more learnedly of what they apprehended and with no greater clearness. Commanders of brigades and divisions looked anxiously to their connections on the right and on the left, sent staff officers on errands of inquiry and pushed skirmish lines silently and cautiously forward into the dubious region between the known and the unknown. (II: 182)

Here, in just three sentences, Bierce captures the essence of the army on that foggy day from its highest to its lowest echelons—a task that would be extremely difficult for one who had not been there and done that. And certainly this is not a task he could have managed without his broadening experience as a staff officer. Here, in this little known Civil War story, is a timeless description of a wartime army in the field.

Most war fiction tends to view a conflict from one perspective. Both the classics *The Red Badge of Courage* and *All Quiet on the Western Front* view the conflict entirely from the perspective of a private soldier. Bierce's war experience, in which he personally viewed the war from a very rare variety of perspectives, allows him to create a uniquely authoritative and accurate narrative voice—one that is able to maintain a sometimes subtle, sometimes not, but altogether verisimilar omniscience. Had Bierce's professional development not included becoming a trusted staff officer of both a brigade and, eventually, a division commander, it is extremely unlikely he could have accomplished such a narrative task. While "One Kind of Officer" is not a great war story, not even one of Bierce's best, what it does demonstrate is his ability to cut across levels of the army with a eye for detail and a similar ability to retell those observations that are, in many ways, more entertaining than the story itself.

Whether Bierce himself was ever put into a situation in which he experienced a duty conflict as dramatic as the one he portrays in "One Kind of Officer" and "Coulter's Notch" is doubtful. If he was, he was uncharacteristically silent about it. There is, however, such an example involving General Hazen, one that Bierce personally witnessed. In May 1888, Bierce published a short memoir called "The Crime at Pickett's Mill" in the *San Francisco Examiner*. The memoir describes a now largely forgotten fight on May 27, 1864, during the campaign for Atlanta.

In the fight at Pickett's Mill, Hazen's badly understrength brigade was pulled out of its position in the Union lines and rapidly moved to the Union's left flank, where it was to be part of an attack designed to locate the Confederate's corresponding flank and turn it so the Union forces could attack the rebels from the rear. The plan called for Hazen's troops to lead the attack with two other brigades (forming four lines of troops) to his immediate rear for support (map 8). Hazen did not care for the plan, as his brigade was already weary from being heavily engaged; to move it and throw it immediately back into action would be a mistake. He expressed this concern to his division commander, General Wood, who, says Hazen, "forestalled any objection on my part" by telling Hazen that he had selected the brigade because he felt it was the unit with "the greatest promise of succeeding in the work at hand" (*Narrative* 256).

To make matters worse, General Wood and the corps commander, General Howard, changed the plan of attack without informing their subordinate commanders and began to commit brigades in a piecemeal succession at roughly forty-five-minute intervals rather than in the massive column formation originally planned. This not only eliminated the possibility of concentrating superior mass at the decisive point, but eliminated any element of surprise that Hazen's Brigade might have enjoyed. Just before the brigade's attack, Wood and Howard were discussing the progress of the operation within earshot of Hazen. Wood commented to Howard, "We will put in Hazen, and see what success he has" (Hazen 257, Bierce I: 283). At that moment Hazen grasped "the true nature of the distinction about to be conferred upon us" (I: 283). Bierce records Hazen's reaction to the revelation:

[W]hen he saw Howard assent—he never uttered a word, rode to the head of his feeble brigade and patiently awaited the command to go.

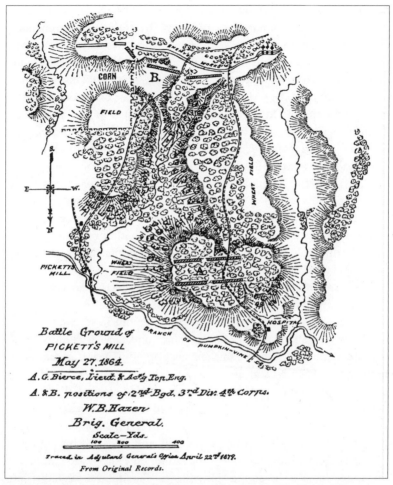

CORN

B.

FIELD

WHEAT FIELD

PICKETT'S MILL

WHEAT FIELD

A.

WHEAT FIELD

HOSPITAL

BRANCH OF PUMPKIN-VINE

Battle Ground of
PICKETT'S MILL
May 27, 1864.
A. G. Bierce, Lieut. & Act'g Top. Eng.
A. & B. positions of 2nd Bgd. 3rd Div. 4th Corps.
W. B. Hazen
Brig. General.
Scale—Yds.
100   200   400
Traced in Adjutant General's Office April 22nd 1879.
From Original Records.

Map 8. Bierce's map of Pickett's Mill From Hazen, *A Narrative of Military Service* (1885; Huntington, WV: Blue Acorn, 1993), facing p. 257.

Only by a look which I knew how to read did he betray his sense of the criminal blunder. (I: 284)

In the ensuing attack, Hazen lost over five hundred men wounded and killed in about thirty minutes of withering Confederate fire. There were no reinforcing lines of troops or artillery to his rear, and the brigade had to fall back to save itself.

One point that emerges from this memoir is the example it provides of Hazen's unflinching sense of duty. Hazen's actions at Pickett's Mill bear some significant resemblance to Coulter's. The key figures, Hazen and Coulter, are commanders of soldiers. In both cases commanders from the next two higher levels of command are physically present at the start of the action and issue questionable orders. Both Hazen and Coulter question, at some point, the order given. There are clear conflicts between a duty to carry out the orders and a duty to preserve one's soldiers, albeit Coulter has the added duty of husband and father in the mix as well. Ultimately, Coulter's reaction is the same as Hazen's. Without speaking a word, Coulter "saluted, and rode straight forward into the Notch" and begins the attack (II: 109).

A key aspect of any junior military officer's professional development is firsthand observation of the actions of senior officers, especially those of an immediate commander or mentor. Given Bierce's role as one of Hazen's understudies, and his unabashed admiration of the general, to see the admirable Captain Coulter react in a similar way to Brigadier General Hazen comes as no surprise.

Bierce wrote one war story that may be set in the late summer of 1863 and follows a pattern of character naming similar to "The Affair at Coulter's Notch." However, the story stands out in several ways as a challenge to the thesis of this book. "Three and One Are One" (1908) is a supernatural tale set on a small family plantation near Carthage, Tennessee. Barr Lassiter, son of the family, left home in 1861 to join the Federal army. Much like Carter Druse in "A Horseman in the Sky," his parents and sister remained staunch Confederates. Now it is about two years later and Lassiter's regiment is camped near his home. The soldier obtains a pass to visit his estranged family and arrives at his old home after dark. As Lassiter approaches the house, his father walks out on the porch and looks at his son in stony silence. Barr follows his father into the house, where he sees his mother and sister, who also look at him, and then completely ignore his presence. His mother and sister leave the room. Discouraged, Lassiter leaves. The next day, he decides to revisit his home. A half mile from his house, he meets a boyhood friend who informs him that about a year before, his house was destroyed by a Union shell that also killed his family.

For this ghost story, Bierce is not as faithful to actual terrain and historical context as he is in "A Baffled Ambuscade" or "A Resumed Identity." However, the setting for this story is not wholly fictional either. Carthage, Tennessee, now better known as the home of former vice president Al Gore, is fifty miles east-northeast of Nashville and about sixty miles north of Manchester. In order to join the Federals, Barr Lassiter made his way to occupied Nashville in 1861, where "he enlisted in the first organization that he found, a Kentucky regiment of cavalry" (III: 351)—a plausible scenario except for the fact that General Buell's advance forces of cavalry did not begin entering Nashville until February 23, 1862, the city having been abandoned by the Confederates for about a week (Losing II: 233–34). The city remained occupied by Federal forces until the end of the war. The narrator goes on to mention twice that it is two years later and Lassiter's regiment is passing through the area of his home in the late summer. If Lassiter enlisted in 1861, then the action of the story would be in 1863. If one insists on complete historical accuracy, based on the actual occupation of Nashville, it would have to be in the late summer of 1864. The principal focus of the Union efforts at the time was Sherman's March to the Sea. However, in September and October of 1864, Confederate General Nathan Bedford Forrest was conducting cavalry raids through middle Tennessee and northern Alabama designed to destroy key railroad facilities and disrupt Sherman's long supply lines. Barr Lassiter's Kentucky cavalry unit could easily be one of the Federal units trying to rid the area of the vexatious Forrest.

Bierce himself was closest to Carthage during the summer of 1863 as Hazen's Brigade moved from Readyville to Manchester. Detailed wartime maps of that area and a letter to Bierce yield what is most likely the only clue to possible sources for this ghost story. On one of the Army of the Cumberland's official maps of the Manchester area dated June 28, 1863, a Lassiter home appears just north of the town. Hazen's Brigade camped at Manchester for a month starting in early to mid-July. Bierce probably encountered the Lassiter name during this stay at Manchester. There was a flurry of mapping activity by the Army of the Cumberland that summer, and Bierce received orders from higher headquarters to map areas all around the Lassiter home. As if to confirm that this is the place he had in mind when he wrote "Three and One Are One," Bierce carries the same spelling (or misspelling) of the family name that appears on Union maps of Manchester. County records show that the family actually spelled its name "Lasater."

Other circumstances make the possibility the story occurs in 1864 even more unlikely. In the late summer of 1864, Bierce returned to Atlanta after recovering from being wounded. Bierce left Atlanta at the end of September or very early October. In October, Bierce was in northern Alabama and did not reenter Tennessee until November. When he did, he went as far north as Nashville in December, then moved with the Fourth Army Corps to winter quarters at Huntsville, Alabama, in

January 1865. The available evidence indicates that he was never near Carthage in 1864.

The Lassiter home Bierce was familiar with was in Manchester, not Carthage. Further, Bierce was never in Carthage for any significant amount of time. One must wonder if this is a possible exception to his general practice of writing about actual places and events that occurred when he was at those places. Moreover, in "A Resumed Identity," "A Baffled Ambuscade," and other ghost stories, Bierce so faithfully locates the action at places without any alterations to those places that this story even calls into question the accuracy of that basic observation. Additionally, the dating seems to be a bit out of step with the historical record—something Bierce just does not do.

The difficulties posed by "Three and One Are One," however, do not call into serious question the assertions posited by this study. As Thomas Foster explains, "'Always' and 'never' are not words that that have much meaning in literary study. [. . .] as soon a something seems to always be true, some wise guy will come along and write something to prove its not" (6). One example of story writing that does not quite fit the pattern serves, if anything, to more strongly demonstrate what a creature of authorial habit Bierce was. Because there is convincing evidence that the Lasater home in Manchester in 1863 was the model for the story, "Three and One Are One" is, fundamentally, another example of the author's adherence to practices evident throughout his war stories. Ambrose Bierce wrote this story late in his career. He first published it in *Cosmopolitan* in 1908, when he was sixty-six. It was the very last war story he published and among his last of any genre. These stories tend to be among his least artistically successful, and it possible that Bierce was diverging from craft practices that had worked for him earlier in his career. It is also very possible that Bierce simply made a mistake when he told the story of Barr Lassiter. He may have simply forgotten that General Buell did not enter Nashville until early 1862; Lassister leaves home in 1861, enlists, and returns two years later. A reader who did not know, or an author who had forgotten, that Nashville was not under Federal control until February 1862 would assume the story takes place in the summer of 1863, the time Bierce was in nearby Manchester. Finally, it is very likely that Bierce moved "Three and One Are One" to Carthage out of simple regard for the family named in it—to avoid having curious readers pester the Manchester Lasaters about ghosts in the family tree. The fact that this story is a singular exception, and not one of several that somehow have to be explained away or ignored to maintain a consistent argument, demonstrates how strong the author's habits were.

Only four and a half months after he originally published the West Virginia story "A Tough Tussle" in the *Examiner*, Bierce published "One Officer, One Man" (1889), a story that, because it involves suicide by sword, has a certain affinity with "A Tough Tussle." "One Officer, One Man" is set in 1863 at a location that cannot be determined with certainty from textual evidence. The story tells of Anderton Graffenreid (whose initials are the same as Bierce's first two and were ones he frequently signed newspaper columns with), a young captain who, to his chagrin, had been assigned an administrative job at the state capital at the war's outset while the rest of his regiment went off to fight. Having dutifully and patiently waited for two years, attrition has at last yielded Graffenreid a position as a company commander in his now combat-hardened regiment. Graffenreid is eager for battle, having endured two years of others' thinking he was cowardly and a shirker for his desk job at the capital. The regiment forms for battle and awaits the order to attack.

Graffenreid's stint away from his regiment provides an important temporal clue to the setting of the story. The war "was two years old," which makes the year 1863 (II: 199). The corps commander's report refers to action on the nineteenth of the month. During that year September 19 immediately comes to mind, as it marks the first day of fighting at Chickamauga. The tactical situation of the story resembles Hazen's own report of action on the eighteenth and early morning of the nineteenth. The title even bears a vague similarity to Hazen's casualty report of the seventeenth, when he reported a loss of "1 captain and several men" (*OR* 1/XXX: 761). There is another vague clue that, if nothing else, at least rules out the story's being set in the winter. As Graffenreid looks out over the ground to his front, he notes the "pleasant landscape with its long stretches of brown fields over which the atmosphere was beginning to quiver in the heat of the morning sun" (II: 198–99). This could certainly describe a very late summer morning in northern Georgia.

Despite its ostensible resemblance to "A Tough Tussle," this story is a study in small-unit leadership and officership that is very consistent with Bierce's other midwar stories. Unlike Second Lieutenant Byring of "A Tough Tussle," Captain Graffenreid does not struggle in isolation in the dark. Graffenreid's actions take place in the full light of day; he is, in fact, at his proper and, in those days, traditional position at the right front of his infantry company. Any isolation that he feels is an internal conflict, a struggle exacerbated in large part by the demands and isolation imposed by Graffenreid's new position of leadership and command.

As Graffenreid stands by his company waiting for the battle to be joined, his thoughts and perceptions become an insightful study in the tensions inherent in small-unit command. Graffenreid has been at an administrative post in the state capital; here at last is the opportunity the good officer has long awaited. Even his fellow officers misunderstand him and think him a shirker. His troops are veterans of many battles and are curious to see how their newcomer commander will fare. He wants, rightfully, to "vindicate his right to the respect of his men and the companionship of his brother officers" (II: 200). All this is going through Graffenreid's mind as he stands waiting for the battle to start. When he dodges a single cannon shot that lands well away from him, "[h]e heard, or fancied he heard, a low mocking laugh" behind him (II: 202). When he turns, he sees his first lieutenant and troops in the front ranks with looks of amusement on their faces, apparently at him. The captain is rapidly becoming unnerved. He feels alone despite the fact his company is formed directly behind him. A volley of enemy rifle fire kills the soldier next to Graffenreid and forces the regiment briefly to lie down for cover. Graffenreid becomes even more unnerved, especially with the dead body next to him. A furious battle begins to rage to the company's right. During the seemingly interminable wait, Graffenreid "sought rather to analyze his feelings than distinguish himself by courage and devotion. The result was profoundly disappointing" (II: 205). Graffenreid realizes he is terrified. The regiment comes to attention and awaits orders to attack that never come. The delay is unbearable, "like a respite at the guillotine" (II: 206). Graffenreid's senses begin to reel. Artistically, this story then has a moment much like Peyton Farquhar experiences as preparations are made for his hanging. Anderton Graffenreid looks at his own officer's saber, with its long, slightly curved blade and sees a sword that, "[f]oreshortened to his view, [. . .] resembled somewhat, he thought, the short heavy blade of the ancient Roman. The fancy was full of suggestion, malign, fateful, heroic!" (II: 207). Graffenreid's fears totally overcome him, and he runs himself through with his own sword, falling forward onto the other dead soldier. A week later, his corps commander recounts the casualty totals for that day in a report. For Graffenreid's unit, the fighting is very light: the total killed is "one officer, one man."

Here is a climactic event very like the one in "A Tough Tussle" but recast in the mind of an officer who is a commander of troops. Much of what makes Graffenreid's cowardice especially appalling to himself is the fact that his display is so public, and in front of the very ones he sought to "vindicate his right to the respect of." Here again are Bierce's concerns about the nature of courage but this time combined with others about leadership and what it means to be an officer. These were not primary concerns of Private or Sergeant Bierce in West Virginia, but they certainly were to First Lieutenant Bierce in late 1863. Here Bierce is following his pattern of setting a story at a time and place when his concerns as a soldier matched thematic ones in the story. Similar to Peyton Farquhar, the narrator so convincingly portrays the leadership concerns in the mind of the young captain that the reader becomes fully engaged and prepared to accept the distorted, even hallucinatory, sensations Graffenreid experiences.

* * *

The summer of 1863 came to an end with the battle of Chickamauga, one of the costliest and most controversial battles of the Civil War. In this battle fought for control of Chattanooga, the Confederate victory was largely Pyrrhic, as the Union ultimately retained control of the besieged city despite losing on the battlefield a few miles away. General Rosecrans had managed to outmaneuver Confederate general Braxton Bragg through central Tennessee and approached, in three columns, what he initially thought was a retreating Bragg. Bragg was in fact attempting to mass to defeat what he thought were two columns of approaching Union troops. In the confused battle in the woods near Chickamauga Creek that followed, Major General Wood's division was mistakenly ordered to pull out of its position on the right of the Federal line (map 9). Wood obediently did so, leaving a gaping hole through which Longstreet's Confederate corps poured. The Union right flank collapsed and began retreating towards Chattanooga. General Rosecrans, thinking his entire army was in retreat, left the field to organize a defense of the city. The Union left flank, under General George "Pap" Thomas reorganized around Snodgrass Hill and held the advancing Confederates, thus preventing a complete Union rout. General Rosecrans was subsequently replaced as commander of the Army of the Cumberland for what his superiors viewed as failures of leadership during the battle.

As in the fights at Shiloh and Stone's River, Hazen's Brigade, which left Poe's Tavern on or about September 10, was in the thick of the action. By the eighteenth the brigade was forming part of the Union line near what was to become the center of the battlefield. When the break in

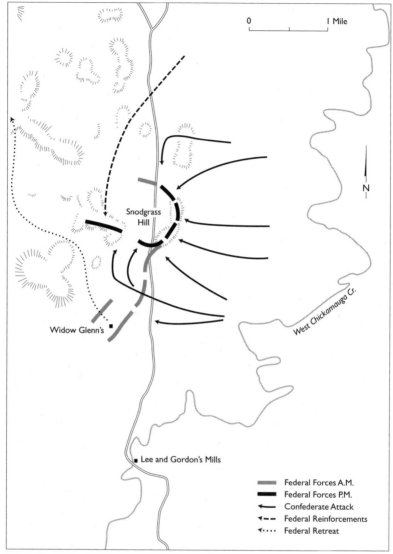

Map 9. The Battle of Chickamauga.

the Federal line occurred, Hazen was just to the left (north) of it and was instrumental in the defense of Snodgrass Hill, the action that earned Thomas the nickname the "Rock of Chickamauga."

The terrain at Chickamauga was far from ideal. Henry Villard, in his postwar memoirs, wrote:

The surface is undulating, and was then generally covered with heavy timber and largely also with an undergrowth so dense that a clear view could be had only for a hundred to two hundred feet. The timber entirely concealed the movements of the hostile forces from one another. There were, however, a number of farms with clearings and cultivated fields of greater or less extent. (112)

These clearings and cultivated fields around small family farms became the major battlefield landmarks. There were few other points of orientation, few other places for artillery to fire from, and, given the individual weaponry and tactics in use, no other places to maneuver and fight. An account of the battle written in 1911 claimed that

a few farms scattered through this woodland were tilled by the obscurest of backwoodsmen, who lived in small log cabins or small frame buildings. Their names would never have been known, even in Chattanooga nine miles away, had it not been for the accidental fighting there of the greatest battle of the west. (Michael Fitch 81)

Much like the fight at Shiloh, the events at Chickamauga inspired Ambrose Bierce to write both a personal memoir and at least one, probably two, short stories based on the battle. The memoir, entitled "A Little of Chickamauga," reflects his familiarity with the terrain around the battlefield, a familiarity evident in his powerful short story "Chickamauga."

Although the terrain of "Chickamauga" (1889) accurately represents that of the actual battlefield, there is an essential point to be made at the outset. Were it not for the title, it would be virtually impossible to locate the action of the story other than its taking place on a small farm in the South. The title, with all its resonance, is the only clear indication of a specific battlefield. Like many other Bierce war stories, it is about the capricious and overwhelming forces of war destroying the protagonist's naïveté. Unlike many others, there are no family or place names of any sort in the text. One could reread the story many times looking for clues, but the specifics given could apply to many southern battlefields at many different times. If the setting could be almost anywhere during the Civil War, then the events could be too, and surely that is a major point of the story.

"Chickamauga" is one of Bierce's most enduring works. The frequency with which it has been anthologized is second only to "An Occurrence at Owl Creek Bridge." It is the story of a nameless young boy's tragic introduction to the harsh realities of war. The boy's father, who is absent from the story, had been a soldier and Indian fighter as a younger man. The boy, armed with a crude wooden toy sword, wanders into the woods near his home. Imagining himself on a grand military adventure like his father's, he becomes lost while running from a rabbit. After falling asleep for a few hours, the child resumes his wanderings. He sees horribly wounded soldiers attempting to reach a stream for water and attempts to ride, horse-style, the back of one who is crawling on hands and knees. While the boy slept, a fierce battle had raged all around him; there had been an attack and a retreat; there are dead bodies in the creek. On the other side of the creek there is a fire glowing somewhere through the woods, and an officer is attempting to rally his soldiers. Attracted to the blaze, the child runs to investigate. Suddenly, he is on familiar ground and he realizes it is his home that is burning. By the light of the flames, he discovers the mangled body of his dead mother and begins "a series of inarticulate and indescribable cries [. . .] a startling, soulless, unholy sound," for the child is a deaf-mute (II: 57).

Because the area of the actual battlefield was so sparsely populated, and the small dwellings and cleared fields became so important to the conduct of the battle, it is relatively simple to account for the families at the Chickamauga battlefield. Although several homes burned, especially those near the center of the fighting, there were no civilian casualties recorded. Most of the families either left the area altogether or hid with their neighbors at "a sort of refugee camp" they established in a ravine northwest of the Reed home. When the fighting got too near, they moved deeper into the woods. For seven days the Snodgrass, Poe, Brotherton, Kelly, McDonald, Brock, and Mullis families hid from the battle. The Vittetoe (frequently misspelled on Union maps) family hid in a large hole under their kitchen floor; fortunately, their house was not destroyed.[5] The Poe, Kelley, Snodgrass, Brotherton, and Glenn families were not as fortunate. They all had homes burned or destroyed by the fighting. Based on Hazen's memoirs, contemporaneous maps, and Bierce's accounts of the battle, the civilian buildings that Hazen's troops (and consequently Bierce) were near were the Kelley, Glenn, Poe, and Snodgrass homes (map 9). Although none of these families lost members to the battle, Bierce's proximity to their ruined houses and his familiarity with the battlefield make them a logical group of possible settings for Bierce's tale.

The only family whose situation has any sort of resemblance to "Chickamauga" is that of Eliza Glenn, more commonly called "Widow Glenn." Widow Glenn's house is most remembered as General Rosecrans's headquarters during the opening day of the battle. When the general arrived and informed her it was necessary for him to take over the home, he advised her to evacuate for her own safety. A slave helped load her few possessions, infant daughter, and two-year-old son into a wagon. He drove the family to the Vittetoe farm and then to her father's farm near Pond Spring. The next day, as the Union right retreated all around the area, a shell struck the house and burned it. Eliza Glenn's deceased husband was not an old soldier and Indian fighter, as is the absent father in Bierce's story, but a Confederate soldier who died of illness in Mobile, Alabama, just two months after enlisting. Her son was two years old, not six.[6]

The creek in Bierce's story may seem a possible clue to a precise battlefield location. Drinking water was indeed a problem, especially for the Union soldiers at Chickamauga. The Confederates could use Chickamauga Creek; for Union soldiers, however, one of the only sources of water was a pond made by a sinkhole very near the Widow Glenn's house. Like the creek that the deaf-mute child sees wounded men attempting to reach, this pond became the scene of similar horrors. Union cavalryman Colonel John H. Wilder recalled that

> neither the men nor horses had water for hours and neither dead men and dead horses nor the blood and mud of Bloody Pond detained them from quenching their agonizing thirst in the pond. Some of them waded into the pond. Others knelt at the edge and drank beside men who had fallen dead of wounds while drinking. (qtd. in Cozzens 394)

The nickname stuck, so that in almost all accounts of the battle the sinkhole is called "Bloody Pond." Not typically mentioned in accounts of the battle, there is also a small, narrow creek running near the sinkhole and the house. The story of the Widow Glenn, though ultimately very different from that of the dead woman at the conclusion of "Chickamauga," has some important similarities to it. She was the mother of a small boy, a battle raged around her house, a shell burned the house, and there was an important source of water nearby. Bierce doubtless knew of at least some of these circumstances. As in "The Affair at Coulter's Notch," Bierce's setting is a composite of elements that appear to be drawn from life, but with a central event and specific location that are his own inventions.

Far-fetched as it may initially sound, Bierce may have chosen to associate this story of virtually any battlefield with the fight at Chickamauga because of an autobiographical element closely associated with Bierce's professional growth. Something happened to the author during this battle that he had not experienced before. Since the time when Bierce became the topographic engineer in April, Hazen's Brigade had not experienced heavy fighting; Chickamauga was the first big battle after Stone's River. Professionally, it was Bierce's first large-scale action as a staff officer. For him, the spring and summer had largely been spent making sometimes dangerous reconnaissance forays and subsequently spending "half the night at my drawing-table, platting my surveys" (II: 209–10). In a battle, however, those sorts of duties fall temporarily by the wayside, and the topographic engineer, like almost any staff officer, becomes a battlefield coordinator and messenger for the commander. Now on horseback for the first time during a battle and no longer a foot soldier, this is exactly what happened to Bierce at Chickamauga.

In his memoir "A Little of Chickamauga," Bierce tells of Hazen sending him to find badly needed artillery ammunition. As he was attempting to return with several wagonloads of it, a large Confederate attack captured the supplies, and Bierce barely escaped. While attempting to make his way back to the brigade, Bierce encountered retreating Union corps commander General James S. Negley. As Bierce tells it, "[M]y duties as topographical engineer having given me some knowledge of the lay of the land[, I] offered to pilot him back to glory or the grave. I am sorry to say my good offices were rejected a little uncivilly" (I: 275). Meanwhile, Hazen's Brigade had moved and Bierce could not find it, but he did find his brother Albert's Ohio artillery battery. Of the incident, Albert Bierce wrote in a 1911 letter, "I remember your saying to me that Hazen had left the position that he held when you left him to go for the ammunition train and as you did not know where he was at the time you would stay with the battery" (Papers). In his memoir, Ambrose explains that as the two chatted, the "incident was a trifle marred" when a Confederate bullet struck another officer of Albert's battery, so the brothers "propped [him] against a tree and left" (I: 276). Not long afterward, Bierce found his brigade near the Snodgrass house. Characteristically, Hazen's first reaction to his long-overdue lieutenant's return was to ask him where the ammunition was. Nonetheless, in his official report on the battle written nine days later, Hazen singled out Bierce and six other staff officers as having been "with me at all times, doing valuable service" and goes on to say that Bierce and three others "deserve special mention" for their actions in the field (OR 1/XXX: 765).

Bierce's memoir is especially significant for two reasons. First, it reflects the familiarity with the Chickamauga battlefield that Bierce developed as a result of his duties. Second, it was the first time during a major battle that he was not an infantryman in an infantry regiment. As part of his official duties at Chickamauga, he was mounted and able to roam over the battlefield taking in a far larger view than had been possible in the past. In this case, of course, he also did considerable wandering when he became separated from the unit. The nature of his duties was now such that he could not take an active role in the fighting. In fact, it would be necessary for him to avoid becoming decisively engaged in order to complete many of his missions. He could, however, see much more of the battlefield than he could possibly have seen as an infantryman, even to the point of seeing other generals in action (or in Negley's case, leaving it) whose commands he was not a part of.

The point now seems fairly obvious that, like the nameless child who wanders the field in the story, Bierce found himself moving around the Chickamauga battlefield, taking in the brutal and sometimes bizarre events. He was, of course, far from being an innocent or naïve observer. But he was learning much about the overall operations of an army in combat and about the impact of various senior officers. Here, perhaps, is why he named the story "Chickamauga."

About a month after Chickamauga, one of the war's strangest events became a source for one of Bierce's most successful spoofs. "Jupiter Doke, Brigadier-General" is unique among the Bierce war stories in that it is the only one told in epistolary fashion.[7] It was Bierce's second Civil War story, originally appearing in *The Wasp* on the day after Christmas 1885. At first, the tale seems so absurd that it could not possibly be based on events to which its author was a personal witness. "Jupiter Doke" is wickedly satirical, certainly in keeping with the tone of many of Bierce's early newspaper and magazine sketches that he collected and republished in *The Fiend's Delight* under the pseudonym Dod Grile.[8]

Through a series of letters, dispatches, newspaper articles, and transcripts, the story describes the military career of a small-time Illinois politician who receives a politically motivated appointment as a brigadier general of volunteers. Doke is so incompetent that his higher-ups try to ensure he is killed or captured by the enemy. So unskilled is he that Doke even has his troops start collecting mules for a retreat, should the enemy attack. Yet he somehow wins a decisive victory over a superior Confederate force and is proclaimed a hero. The last segment of the story is a statement from a slave who recounts that on the night the Confederates were massing for an attack, he woke Doke, who ran for the mule yard and so frightened the animals that they stampeded down the road the Rebels were forming on and annihilated the advancing enemy.

Absurd as it is, Bierce based "Jupiter Doke" on an actual incident. The incident was part of the Battle of Wauhatchie, Tennessee, in late

October 1863 and is generally known as the "Charge of the Mule Brigade." In the early morning hours of October 27, Hazen's Brigade was part of a large Federal force that made a daring trip down the Tennessee River by boats under cover of darkness and fog to seize the key river crossing site at Brown's Ferry (map 2). Federal engineers quickly threw a pontoon bridge across the river to Chattanooga in order to get needed supplies and men to the besieged city. The next night, Confederate forces counterattacked at Wauhatchie, about four miles south of the bridge site and deep behind Union lines. Union teamsters, panicked by the attack, abandoned their mules, which, terrified at the heavy fire, stampeded directly into the attacking Confederates. In the ensuing confusion, the Confederates, who had superior numbers, thought they were under a heavy cavalry attack and retreated. According to historian E. B. Long, by 4:00 A.M. "the confused engagement ended," and it was "one of the few fairly important night engagements of the war" (427). Thanks to the mules, the Union scored a clear victory despite heavier losses. According to Roy Morris, the story of the mule stampede quickly spread through both armies and even made it to the troops fighting in Virginia (68). Exactly where Bierce was during the fight at Wauhatchie is unknown. He was probably with Hazen (who claimed that the Confederate attack was "meant for us") at Brown's Ferry, about four or five miles from the stampeding mules (*Narrative* 163).[9]

Morris is certainly correct in his pronouncement that "Jupiter Doke" "takes numerous barely concealed digs" at Ulysses S. Grant (70). Doke's first name, state, and Republican Party affiliation mirror Grant's. Doke even includes a line in his letter accepting his appointment that Grant also used in his first inauguration speech in 1869. More tellingly, the names of two of the Confederate generals whom Doke unwittingly defeats, Gibeon Buxter and Dolliver Billows, poke fun at Confederates Gideon Pillow and Simon Bolivar Buckner, two of the generals whom Grant defeated during the capture of Forts Henry and Donelson. To bolster Morris's case a bit more, it is worth noting that the date of Doke's great victory is February 2, 1862—the day before Grant launched his forces for the Henry-Donelson campaign.

G. Thomas Couser has also noted that "Jupiter Doke" lampoons the process by which history is recorded. Each recorder tends to color events, often to put himself in the best possible light. Certainly this view is consistent with what Bierce himself says about history and historians in *The Devil's Dictionary*. History is an "account mostly false, of events mostly unimportant, which are brought about by rulers mostly knaves, and soldiers, mostly fools." A historian is simply a "broad-gauge gossip" (VII: 138). Cathy N. Davidson offers another important approach when she reads "Jupiter Doke" as a study "on the nature of confusion and delusion in attempted communication" and makes special note of the irony in the fact that the only accurate account of the so-called battle comes from a man who is "uneducated, illiterate, and almost blind" (*Experimental* 72, 75).

Criticism of "Jupiter Doke" does emphasize the point that Bierce's second war story is one of his best. Doubtless some of the reason for this success is that he was especially well qualified to tell it. Beyond his proximity to the event that he based the story on, Bierce's experience as a newspaper columnist adds an important dimension to the story. When the story first appeared in the *Wasp*, Bierce was well established as a caustic wit whom some called "the *Wasp* stinger" (Morris 193). Bierce directed much of his print invective at local San Francisco political figures—the same sorts of characters as Doke. One of the funniest bits of the story is the editorial column from the Posey, Illinois, *Maverick* that characterizes Doke as "the Great Captain who made the history as well as wrote it," probably another dig at Grant and his recently published memoirs (VIII: 32–33). Bierce is especially good at lampooning such columns because he was very familiar with writing them as well.

Letters and dispatches between Doke, his commander, and the secretary of war form the bulk of "Jupiter Doke," and it is here that Bierce's military experience comes into play. Once again, the ancillary duties that were inherent in his position as an officer of Hazen's personal staff are significant. In addition to mapmaking duties and the battlefield coordination and messenger duties mentioned in the discussion of "Chickamauga," Bierce frequently wrote, read, and delivered correspondence and orders on behalf of his commander. As such, he became intimately familiar with the sometimes overblown, often all-too-deferential, and sometimes hyperbolic language of such dispatches. In October 1863, for example, when General Hazen requested that Bierce and a surgeon be allowed to remain in the brigade rather than being transferred all the way to Army of the Cumberland headquarters, a staff officer at division headquarters penned the following endorsement to Hazen's request before sending it up the chain of command:

> General—I am instructed by General Palmer to say that he has a high appreciation of both the officers named, considering them among the very best in the service. Yet entertaining a sincere desire to gratify and

accommodate both them and you—your request is most cheerfully complied with. (Starling)

Another example is the following, from a staff officer in one of the regiments in Hazen's Brigade describing a failed movement on a very wet, dark night during the summer of 1863:

> Having succeeded in getting the [horse-drawn supply wagons] successfully on the big hill, the regiment, in company with the [wagons], moved forward, stopping at 2 o'clock at night. The roads being in such condition and the moon having gone down—the night was as dark as a Rebel's conscience—it was impossible to move further without the benefit of daylight. (qtd. in Hewett 217)

Yet another is this passage in a letter from Congressman William Morrow of California to Bierce in July 1886 to Bierce, when Bierce, with Hazen's assistance, was attempting to correct a problem with service dates on a pension application. The congressmen seems especially concerned with efficiently responding to a request from his well-known constituent at the *Wasp*:

> I called yesterday upon the Assistant Adjutant General and requested that he should make an examination of your record [. . .]. [The Army's chief of personnel] made the matter special and has promised to report to me on next Monday, when I will advise you as to the result. I will take great pleasure in serving you in this or any other matter before the Department of the Government to the best of my ability and influence.
>
> I had a very pleasant interview with General Hazen the other day, in which he spoke of you very kindly and asked very particularly about your welfare.

Unfortunately, there are no extant examples of such dispatches penned by Bierce, but he certainly read and delivered many. It comes as no surprise then, that much of the effectiveness of "Jupiter Doke, Brigadier-General" comes from satirizing the sorts of correspondence with which Bierce, by the end of 1863, had become so familiar. This passage, for example, is from Doke's letter to the secretary of war accepting the commission he has been offered:

> I accept the great trust confided in me by a free and intelligent people, and with a firm reliance on the principles of constitutional liberty, and invoking the guidance of an all-wise Providence, Ruler of Nations, shall

labor so to discharge it as to leave no blot on my political escutcheon. (VIII: 24)

In the end, "Jupiter Doke" is a story that serves as a bridge for Bierce between his military, journalistic, and literary worlds. In his second war story, he successfully links his past life as a soldier, his ongoing life as a journalist, and his emerging future as a war story author.

Still in the wake of Chickamauga and four weeks after the mules' charge, there was another remarkable battle in store for Hazen's Brigade at the close of 1863. Again, Bierce was in the thick of things during the fight for Missionary Ridge, carrying tactical orders from Hazen to units in the brigade as he did during the Battle of Chickamauga. The battle was a decisive Union victory that both settled the issue of who controlled Chattanooga and set the stage for the campaign for Atlanta the following year. The extremely steep ridgeline was the center of Confederate positions that were continuing to lay siege to Chattanooga after the fight at Chickamauga. Grant ordered an attack on Confederate positions at the base of the ridge in response to what he mistakenly thought was an enemy buildup there. When the Federals overran the positions, they were quickly subjected to withering fire from strong Confederate positions at the top. There was no place for the Union troops to go but up, and in a spontaneous, uncoordinated, and unordered attack, regiments and brigades began charging up Missionary Ridge. Despite an overwhelming advantage of position, the Confederates retreated, and the Union had at last gained full control of Chattanooga.

Here again, Hazen's Brigade played a key role in the battle. Although still a matter of controversy, it is safe to say the brigade was one of the very first to reach the top of the ridge.[10] Bierce's presence at the event is confirmed by an officer of the Sixth Kentucky Infantry who reported: "[T]he enemy fleeing in front of us, a part of the regiment was sent to the right, by order of Lieutenant Bierce, of General Hazen's staff" (qtd. in Morris 73). This new role of lone horseman moving about the battlefield would increasingly find its way into Bierce's war fiction and become a primal motif for his fiction set in 1864.

Appropriately enough, 1863 closed with the Ninth Indiana, including Bierce, returning to Indiana for a two-month furlough and mustering in again in February 1864. It had clearly been the most significant year of the war for Lieutenant Ambrose Bierce. His passage from "the droopy, indifferent, studiedly world-weary teenager who [. . .] left for the front in April 1861" to the young officer "with the bristling blond mustache who returned home to Warsaw on furlough in mid-December 1863" was complete, and the stories he wrote about events of that time reflect the essential circumstances and concerns of that transformation (Morris 74). In particular, his stories about the nature of being an officer demonstrate his greatly increased level of professional maturity.

Chapter 5

Late War Stories

1864, to Atlanta and Franklin

COWARD, *n*. One who in a perilous emergency thinks with his legs.
VALOR, *n*. A soldierly compound of vanity, duty and the gambler's hope.

The Devil's Dictionary

"Cowardice" means a shrinking from danger, not a shirking of duty.

Ambrose Bierce
"Taking Oneself Off" (1912)

Among these [dead] were so many good men who could ill be spared from the army and the world. And yet I am left. But my turn will come in time.

Bierce
in a letter to Clara Wright, June 8, 1864

In the spring of 1864, the Army of the Cumberland, which still included Hazen's Brigade and the newly reenlisted Ninth Indiana Volunteers, became a part of General William T. Sherman's campaign for Atlanta. In early May, Sherman began pushing out of the Chattanooga area and northwestern Georgia and pushing toward Atlanta along the route of what is now Interstate Highway 75 (map 10). Ambrose Bierce based at

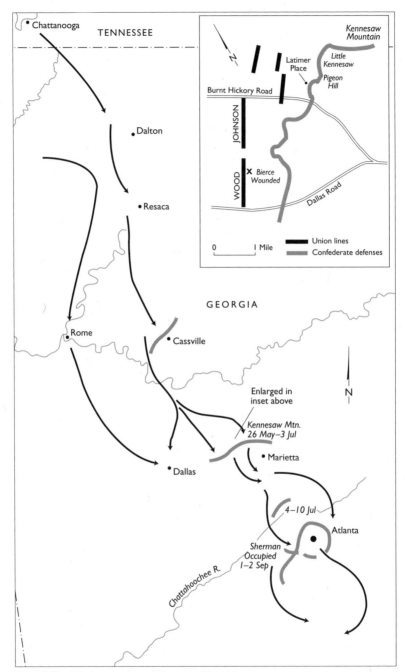

Map 10. The Atlanta campaign and Kennesaw Mountain.

least three of his works on the Atlanta campaign: the memoir "The Crime at Pickett's Mill" and two short stories, "Killed at Resaca" and "One of the Missing."

The battle at Resaca was one of the first significant fights of the Atlanta campaign. It took place from May 13 to May 16 about halfway between Chattanooga and Marietta, Georgia. For the Confederates, it was one of a series of unsuccessful attempts to stop Sherman's movement toward Atlanta. While the fighting raged at Resaca, Sherman was able to move a large number of troops around the Rebel positions there, consequently forcing the Confederates to abandon the fight, move farther south, and reestablish positions to block the Union drive.

"Killed at Resaca" (1887), an account of the death of First Lieutenant Herman Brayle, establishes another of Bierce's primal scenes and a theme that he explores in several subsequent stories. This primal scene, the one that appears to have had its genesis in the events of Chickamauga and Missionary Ridge, is not the lone sentry at some outpost but a lone officer on horseback making a courageous gallop against seemingly impossible odds. It is a motif that Bierce uses to explore the nature of individual courage in a way that stories set earlier in the war do not. The officer or soldier of the line typically demonstrates his courage by the way he leads his soldiers in the face of the enemy or the way he engages the enemy himself. The staff officer, however, has no soldiers to lead, nor does he typically engage the enemy directly. As a result, at least in Bierce's stories, how he reacts in the face of the enemy becomes the public demonstration of his courage.

Lieutenant Brayle is a dashing, well-liked aide-de-camp to a Union general. The first-person narrator, who is the unit's topographer, claims Brayle has but one "objectionable and unsoldierly quality: he was vain of his courage" (II: 94). Brayle frequently exposes himself needlessly to enemy fire, and he virtually refuses to seek cover when under fire. The young lieutenant finally meets his end at the battle of Resaca, Georgia. Told by the general to take a message to an adjacent unit's commander, Brayle rides forward of the Union lines through a cleared field instead of taking the longer, safer route through the woods to the rear. Brayle rides parallel to the enemy's earthworks less than two hundred yards from them. Confederate rifles and artillery begin firing at the lone horseman. Suddenly, Brayle halts. The narrator immediately knows the reason: as the brigade's topographic engineer, he had made a reconnaissance earlier in the day and found "a deep and sinuous gully" to Brayle's immediate front, one that cannot be seen from the Union lines (II: 101). Brayle will neither take cover in the ditch nor turn around. The gallant lieutenant is quickly gunned down. A team of litter bearers, carrying a white flag, move onto the field to retrieve the body. Several Confederates meet them and reverently assist with loading Brayle's remains onto a stretcher. From behind the Confederate lines, fifes and drums play a dirge in tribute. Once his body is recovered, the general orders Brayle's possessions distributed, and the narrator inherits Brayle's leather-bound pocket notebook.

The time shifts to 1866. The narrator is on his way to California and discovers a letter in the notebook from a woman. It is a love letter from Brayle's sweetheart in San Francisco. Written in July of 1862, the letter explains that she has heard that at a battle in Virginia, Brayle was seen "crouching behind a tree." She goes on to say "I could bear to hear of my soldier lover's death, but not of his cowardice." The narrator calls on the lady one evening and finds her "beautiful, well bred—in a word, charming." He explains that he is there to return the letter to her. She thanks him and, while looking at the letter, gives a sudden start. She asks if the stain on the letter is blood. The narrator explains that it "is the blood of the truest and bravest heart that ever beat." Repulsed, she flings the letter in the fire claiming she cannot bear the sight of blood. When she asks how Brayle died, the narrator replies, "He was bitten by a snake" (II: 103–4).[1]

Carey McWilliams reads "Killed at Resaca" as pure autobiography, right down to the visit to the young lady on Rincon Hill in San Francisco. However, McWilliams offers no support for such a reading, and he appears to have committed a mistake that is fairly common in much Bierce biography and criticism, namely assuming that because so many elements of a Bierce war story are autobiographical, all of them must be. There is no evidence to support the existence of a Lieutenant Herman Brayle. If, as McWilliams believes, Brayle was a member of Hazen's staff, then his name would be expected to appear somewhere in *A Narrative of Military Service* and in official records. After all, Hazen claims his purpose in writing his book is "a duty which I owed to my men [. . .] to tell the story of our common service. [. . .] It may make a son's heart exult at the sight of his father's name" (v–vi). Indeed, Hazen seems to include as many names of the meritorious as he possibly can on each page, yet Brayle is not among those cited. Neither Hazen nor anyone else mentions similar incidents in accounts of the battle at Resaca. Nor is Brayle's name in Army of the Cumberland records. Brayle, it appears, is an invented name.

Certainly it is also possible that the central event of the story might be inspired by actual events even if the protagonist's name is fictitious. Interestingly enough, topography seems to rule out such a possibility. Brayle's fate is closely tied to a terrain feature, the "deep and sinuous gully, crossing half the field from the enemy's line," which the narrator had seen earlier in the day (II: 101). The gully, like Coulter's Notch or the cliff in "A Horseman in the Sky," is essential to the story. If such a topographic feature exists, it lends credence to McWilliams's reading; if it does not, then the account of Brayle's fate in "Killed at Resaca" is probably purely fictional. During the battle, Bierce prepared a detailed map of Hazen's position at Resaca (map 11). The map illustrates the ground the narrator describes when he reports, "In front of our brigade the enemy's line of earthworks ran through open fields along a slight crest. At each end of this open ground we were close up to him in the woods, but the clear ground we could not hope to occupy until night" (II: 98). The enemy earthworks along the crest and the open ground to Hazen's front (east) are evident on Bierce's map. The map also shows two clumps of trees and two roads leading to Resaca in front of the brigade. However, even with such detail, Bierce does not show the "clearly impassable" gully. An impassable gully leading from the enemy's lines halfway across the fields to the Union lines would be a significant terrain feature, one that, if it existed, Ambrose Bierce, the meticulous cartographer whose maps were "accurately drawn [. . .] on the spot" would be unlikely to omit (Hazen, *Narrative* 257). The portion of the Resaca battlefield occupied by Hazen's Brigade still remains substantially as it was during the battle. Bierce's map is still easy to follow on the ground, and there is not a gully on the ground that Lieutenant Brayle would have made his gallant ride across.[2] Brayle's ride may have some basis in fact, but his fate is a Bierce invention.

Much as it might resemble Bierce's own actions at Chickamauga and Missionary Ridge, the brave lieutenant's dash has an even stronger autobiographical precedent. In a newspaper column for the *Wasp* on July 14, 1883, Bierce wrote of a personal experience that occurred in very late 1864. He was briefly on the staff of division commander General Samuel Beatty and was once required to guide the division's reserve forces into a position to assist one of its brigades. There was not time to conduct a

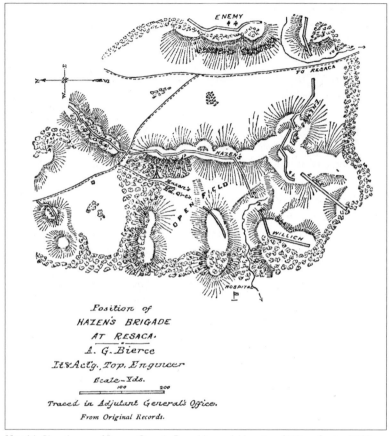

Map 11. Bierce's map of Resaca, Georgia. From Hazen, *A Narrative of Military Service* (1885; Huntington, WV: Blue Acorn, 1993), facing p. 251.

proper reconnaissance along the route, so Lieutenant Bierce rode ahead of the column. Recalling the events in the newspaper, he writes:

> I never felt so brave in all my life. I rode a hundred yards in advance, prepared to expostulate single handed with the victorious enemy at whatever point I might encounter him. I dashed forward through every open space into every suspicious looking wood and spurred to the crest of every hill, exposing myself recklessly to draw the Confederate fire and disclose their position. I told the commander of the relief column that he need not throw out any advance guard as a precaution against the ambuscade—I would myself act in that perilous capacity.

Doubtless this experience, combined with similar ones in late 1863, help explain the actions of Lieutenant Brayle.

In addition to the *Wasp* column and "Killed at Resaca," the lone rider would appear in another war story, entitled "A Son of the Gods" (1888). At least two critics, McWilliams and Woodruff, believe Bierce drew heavily on his experience under General Beatty in "A Son of the Gods." It tells the story of an extraordinarily dashing young officer's daring and sacrificial ride in front of suspected enemy positions in order to draw fire and cause the enemy to disclose his location and strength. The officer, whom the narrator calls "this military Christ," makes the ultimate sacrifice so that a line of skirmishers does not have to be sent to perform the deadly task (II: 65). The narrator describes the ride:

> He is riding at a walk, straight up the long slope, with never a turn of his head. How glorious! Gods! [. . .] He does not draw his sabre; his right hand hangs easily at his side. The breeze catches the plume in his hat. [. . .] Straight on he rides. [. . .]   [. . .] If the enemy has not retreated he is in force on that ridge. [. . .] Our horseman, now within a quarter of a mile of the crest, suddenly wheels to the left and gallops in a direction parallel to it. He has caught sight of the antagonist. [. . . Horse and rider] are making directly to our left, parallel to the now steadily blazing and smoking wall. The rattle of the musketry is continuous. [. . .] Enchanted horse and rider have passed a ravine and are climbing another slope. [. . .]
> [. . .] The horse rears and strikes the air with its forefeet. They are down at last. (II: 62–68)

As critics have properly noted, this highly romanticized scene bears remarkable similarities to the personal experience Bierce described in his 1883 article. But Bierce himself raised another possibility when he commented specifically on this story in an *Examiner* column in 1897. A critic had opined, "It is a great thing to watch the 'Son of the Gods' ride out to his sure death like a stage hero. It is magnificent, but it is not war" (qtd. by Bierce, 1 Mar 1897). Bierce responded, "Well, I saw that thing done, just as related. True, the 'Son' escaped whole, but he 'rode out' all right, and if matters had been as we all believed them to be, and as he thought them himself, he would have been shot to rags." Here Bierce is confirming that he saw something like the gallant ride actually happen and that the rider, unlike Herman Brayle or the son of the gods, survived because the Confederates were not where they were thought to be. This brief mention of a lone horseman in the *Examiner* bears such resemblance to Bierce's own gallant ride that one wonders if the rider Bierce mentions in this column is, in fact, himself. It is an idea that seems even more plausible because Bierce concluded his column for the *Wasp* years before by explaining that his ride had been largely in vain because "there had been a misunderstanding" about the enemy's presence.

"Killed at Resaca" repeats the same fundamental vignette, though the point seems to have escaped critical notice. The narrator describes the lieutenant's heroic ride:

> Brayle had cantered lightly into the field.
>
> [. . . He] was beyond recall, galloping easily along, parallel to the enemy and less than two hundred yards distant. He was a picture to see! His hat blown or shot from his head. [. . .] He sat erect in the saddle [. . .] his right hand hanging carelessly at his side. [. . .] Successive scores of rifles spat at him as he came within range. [. . .] I instantly saw what had stopped him.
>
> [. . .] At that point was a deep and sinuous gully. [. . .] Clearly, it was impassable. [. . .] He stood awaiting death. It did not keep him long waiting. (II: 99–101)

Although Brayle's reason for riding forth is different (he is delivering a message instead of attempting to locate enemy positions), the similarities between the three events, even down to the appearance of a ravine in the two war stories, indicates they are retellings of the author's ride.

Bierce's narrative technique is the most significant difference among the three vignettes. In the newspaper article, Bierce recalls his own experience in the first person. In "A Son of the Gods," the point of view is first-person plural with occasional shifts to second person. To add to this unusual narration, the story is told in the present tense, an element highlighted in the story's subtitle, "A Study in the Present Tense." In "Killed at Resaca," the narration is in a first-person retrospective voice. The fact that Bierce writes all three versions using some variation of first-person narration further reinforces the autobiographical nature of the incident. The single feature of Bierce's fiction that has consistently drawn much critical comment is his experimentation with narrative technique. These three tellings of the young officer's brave ride are examples of that sort of experimentation.

"A Son of the Gods," then, helps demonstrate that "Killed at Resaca" is not, as McWilliams believes, an account of something the author witnessed in May 1864 and had a hand in after the war. However, it is autobiographical in a complex and extraordinary sense; Ambrose Bierce is telling a story through the voice of a topographic engineer at Resaca (which he was) about a young lieutenant's bold actions in the face of danger (which he had performed and may also have witnessed). The terrain of the setting, which Bierce describes with his customary eye for detail, also contains the invented feature that rules out the story as a factual account. There was not a gully at Resaca.

"George Thurston: Three Incidents in the Life of a Man" (1883) is similarly rich in autobiographical detail. Although it is Bierce's first published war story, its place in this study comes very late for three reasons: a contextual link, a character link, and a late thematic concern. First, "George Thurston" opens with a situation almost identical to Bierce's captivity narrative "Four Days in Dixie" (1888), set in northeastern Alabama in October 1864. In the former, the narrator is, once again, the brigade topographic engineer and explains how Thurston came to join the staff of a Federal brigade:

> Colonel Brough was only temporarily in command, as senior colonel, the brigadier-general having been severely wounded and granted a leave of absence to recover. [. . .] One morning as I set out at the head of my escort on an expedition of more than usual hazard Lieutenant Thurston rode up alongside and asked if I had any objection to his accompanying me, the colonel commanding having given him permission. (II: 209, 211)

In the captivity memoir, Bierce explains:

> I was on the staff of Colonel McConnell, who commanded an infantry brigade in the absence of its regular commander. McConnell was a good man, but he did not keep a very tight rein upon the half dozen restless and reckless young fellows who (for our sins) constituted his "military family." In most matters we followed the trend of our desires, which commonly ran in the direction of adventure. (I: 297–98)

In both works, an acting commander temporarily commands an infantry brigade, the narrator is the topographic engineer, and the narrator and another "reckless young" staff officer set off on some type of adventure. Although "George Thurston" gives no clues to the time and place of its setting, based on the autobiographic touches, it seems reasonable to assume it is roughly the same time as "Four Days in Dixie"—late 1864.

Second, a character in the George Thurston story provides another autobiographical connection. One of the narrator's fellow staff officers is a quartermaster who is "an irreclaimable stammerer when the wine was in" (II: 214). This same unnamed stammering quartermaster appears again in "Killed at Resaca," a story easily placed in May 1864. The problem is that during the battle at Resaca, Bierce was on Hazen's staff, but by late 1864, the time of "Four Days in Dixie," Bierce was on the staff of Colonel McConnell, who was filling in for Colonel Sidney Post. Unlike the brigadier general in "George Thurston," Hazen was never wounded. It appears then that Bierce used situations from his days on both staffs to provide a scenario for the short story. The larger point, however, is that whichever staff Bierce may be drawing upon, he was on both during the year 1864.

Finally, the dominant thematic concern in "George Thurston" is the nature of courage in an individual officer, a point entirely consistent with Bierce's other works associated with 1864. Like Herman Brayle and the nameless son of the gods, George Thurston is a staff officer quite concerned with how others perceive his level of individual courage. Thurston is a rather aloof and "unsocial" figure among his fellow staff officers, and some dislike him (II: 209). The narrator comes to have a grudging respect for him after Thurston displays extraordinary coolness in the face of what seems certain death on the mapping expedition. Unarmed and alone, his horse having been mortally wounded, Thurston simply folds his arms across his chest as a Confederate cavalryman bears down on him with saber drawn. A few weeks later, Thurston makes a similar display. During an attack in dense woods, he becomes separated from his unit and inadvertently walks into an entire company of Confederate infantry, who level their rifles at him as their commander demands he drop his sword and surrender. Thurston calmly refuses and once again crosses his arms across his chest. Several of the rebels shoot him; others are too taken aback to fire. He survives the wounding and rejoins his unit after a period of convalescence. Months later when the unit is in camp, some soldiers attach a playground-style swing to a limb of a tall tree. Thurston takes his turn in the fun and, though new to the business, swings higher than anyone else. Onlookers attempt to warn him of the danger, but Thurston manages to swing as high as the branch, the rope slackens, and he makes a spectacular plummet to his death. His neck is broken, he has a compound fracture of one leg, his abdomen is burst, but, characteristically, his "arms were folded tightly across the breast" (II: 217).

Roy Morris writes that this is a story about suicide, but Thurston's death is ambiguous. While it is true that the protagonist's efforts to show himself courageous border on the suicidal, it is not clear that what he does is with the intent of killing himself. The narrator introduces the ambiguity when he explains that at the critical moment, "Thurston and the swing had parted—that is all that can be known; both hands at once had released the rope" (II: 216). A similar, even stronger case can be made for the story's being about the nature of courage. At one point, the topographer and the quartermaster speculate about what causes Thurston to act the way he does. The former thinks that Thurston's remarkable capability of "tranquilly looking death in the eye and refusing him any concession" causes the lieutenant to have a high opinion of himself and consequently a "stiffish attitude" (II: 214). The latter, and probably the more astute, opines that Thurston's actions are his way of mastering a constitutional tendency to run away (the flight response in the language of later psychology), which means he is not a coward because if he were, he would not even try to master it. There is no foreshadowing hint in the story that Thurston's actions are the result of a suicidal death wish, something one would expect given Bierce's typical practices—even "An Occurrence at Owl Creek Bridge" is rife with clues about what is really happening to Farquhar long before the memorable last sentence of the story. Surely if this were a tale about suicide, the reader would be subtly forewarned.

Less than two weeks after Resaca, as Sherman continued to drive on Atlanta, came the fight at Pickett's Mill and the devastating casualties to Hazen's Brigade mentioned in the previous chapter. Less than three weeks after Pickett's Mill, Hazen's Brigade became a part of the battle for Kennesaw Mountain, just north of Marietta, Georgia. The battle for Kennesaw began in mid-June and concluded on the twenty-seventh. Kennesaw would be an extremely costly fight for the Union; the Confederates occupied a series of breastworks, the last of which were long trenches on the crests of Big and Little Kennesaw Mountains and Pigeon Hill. Confederate artillery had outstanding fields of fire from several positions on these hills. Benson J. Lossing described the Confederate artillery on Big and Little Kennesaw: "Batteries covered their summits. [. . .] From this lofty height, [Confederate General Johnston] could look down upon the entire host of his antagonist, and his batteries could hurl terrible plunging shot and shell" (III: 378–80). As the Union army approached, the rebels fought delaying actions until pushed into their final line of defenses along the mountaintops. General Hazen's account of the initial days of the battle tells of a series of advances, normally made during the early morning, followed by construction of hasty breastworks for protection. During such an operation on June 23, Hazen noted, "Lieutenant Bierce, acting topographical engineer, wounded in the head" (*Narrative* 264). Bierce, while performing one of the sort of ancillary duties required of a staff officer, was coordinating the advance of Hazen's skirmish line when he was hit by a Confederate sharpshooter.

At the time, Hazen's Brigade was between the Burnt Hickory and Dallas roads about one and one-half miles west of the intersection of those roads (map 10). Paul Fatout, one of Bierce's most reliable biographers, claims that Bierce's brother Albert tended to the wound after Ambrose was given up for dead. Thanks to Albert's first aid, Bierce survived and was sent home to Indiana to recuperate (*Lexicographer* 54).

"One of the Missing" (1888) is a story about the death of Jerome Searing, a Union soldier at Kennesaw Mountain. Contrary to what one might expect, other than the location and the fact that both men had a brother nearby, the story has very few similarities to Bierce's wounding. Searing is sent ahead of his unit's lines to scout the enemy. He takes cover in an outbuilding of a deserted plantation and watches a column of retiring Confederates one-half mile away straining up a road on a spur of Kennesaw Mountain. Searing decides to test his marksmanship and take a shot at the column. As Searing prepares to fire his rifle, a Confederate artillery captain, waiting to begin moving up the mountain, fires a cannon at what he thinks is a group of Federal officers standing on a hill. The artillery shell misses and crashes into the building that conceals Searing. He is not seriously injured but is trapped by the rubble of the building. His rifle is also caught in the wreckage and is pointed straight at his forehead. Unable to free himself, Searing realizes he is "caught like a rat in a trap—in a trap, trap, trap" (II: 79). Searing cannot stand the sight of the rifle pointed at his head; his senses seem amplified, time becomes distorted, and thoughts of his family and of his own youth go through his mind. Searing's head begins to throb. He thinks of rats in the building eating away at him. He becomes increasingly terrified. Finally, he manages to free one hand and grab a small strip of board. He is able to place one end of the board against the rifle's trigger and pushes with all his might. The rifle does not fire; unknown to Searing, it had discharged when the shell landed. But Searing dies from the sheer terror of the situation. Meanwhile, Searing's brother Adrian, a Union lieutenant, begins to advance with a line of pickets. He glances at his watch when he hears the cannon shell land; it is 6:18. Adrian moves forward and shortly comes to the plantation where his brother lies. He glances in the ruined outbuilding and sees a yellowish corpse in a uniform so dusty it appears to be Confederate. Its face is so contorted that Adrian does not recognize Jerome. "Dead a week," he remarks and checks his watch again; it is 6:40 (II: 92).

Historically, the action described in the story corresponds very well with events of June 17 or 18. The seemingly random time of Searing's death at 6:18 might even serve as an encoded indication of the month and date inserted by the author. In Bierce's tale, there is an early-morning reconnaissance by scouts and pickets, both sides occupy dug-in positions, and the Union commanders want to press forward, circumstances that reflect the same type of activities Hazen describes in the days just prior to Bierce's wounding. In fact, on the night of the June 16, the Confederates began pulling out of their trench lines that ran roughly parallel to Burnt Hickory Road in front of Kennesaw Mountain. They retreated up the mountains, pulling their artillery with great effort, and occupied their final line of defenses along the mountain crests. Early on the morning of June 18, the Federals gained possession of the Confederate trenches.[3] This appears to be the larger action of which Jerome Searing is part. Having been sent to determine if the enemy has withdrawn, he crosses deserted Confederate positions, then watches "the rear guard of the retiring enemy" as they go "toiling up the mountain road" on Kennesaw Mountain (II: 75).

If Bierce thought of an extant homesite as the place of Searing's death, then the most likely candidate is the Latimer Place, a small plantation that still stands near Burnt Hickory Road and that was alongside the abandoned Confederate trench line (map 11). The other possibility is the Hardage house, which was destroyed. Searing watches Confederates on "a spur of Kennesaw Mountain, a half-mile away" (II: 75). Both these structures stood within a half mile of what is now called the Kennesaw Spur and at the time was known as Pigeon Hill. They are also within two miles of the site where Bierce was wounded.

The setting of "One of the Missing" has strong similarities to that of "Chickamauga." Both stories occur on well-known battlefields and involve civilian homes that may not have existed but appear to be at least drawn in part from actual dwellings at those battlefields. The protagonists of both stories enter dark, ominous forests and then emerge at the war-ravaged home where a terrifying epiphany into the nature of war and death occurs. These common elements of both settings highlight the thematic affinities between the two stories as well. Jerome Searing is a very competent and skilled soldier at the start of the story; the unnamed boy of "Chickamauga" fancies himself as such. At some point, time becomes distorted for both characters; the boy sleeps while a battle rages, Searing is trapped for twenty-two minutes that seem like days. Finally, circumstances beyond their control create a shattering emotional experience for both. For the young deaf-mute, his mother's death is a loss of innocence and an introduction to the realities of war. For Jerome

Searing, "the man of courage, the formidable enemy, the strong, resolute warrior" already familiar with the horrors of war, his predicament is an introduction to personal terror (II: 88). Ironically, as he lays trapped, Searing's final recollections are of his childhood. He is, in the end, as helpless as the young child and able to take only one action, which just as ironically, fails.

This story reflects a benchmark in Bierce's professional development, one inextricably linked to his wounding. While "Killed at Resaca" and "George Thurston" deal with individual courage demonstrated, "One of the Missing" is a story about individual courage overwhelmed. In many ways, it is a return to West Virginia. Searing is a private who, in the isolation of the ruined outbuilding, must make an extraordinary moral decision, namely to kill himself rather than continue to face the ominous rifle barrel. This story has a quality of coming full circle about it, of, at the site of Bierce's wounding where everything almost ended for him, returning to the sort of lone-soldier primal scene he started the war with. The temptation here, which this examination resists, is to lapse into an armchair psychoanalysis of the author and speculate about the mental trauma associated with his wounding somehow being akin to that of originally entering the war. Yet there is a rather clear transition in tone and theme of Ambrose Bierce's war stories that begins here. If the West Virginia stories are marked by the quality of wonder at the start of something, then "One of the Missing" and the works that follow it have the unmistakable air of bringing something to a close.

Something very important was indeed coming to a close for Bierce when he was wounded, namely his wartime association with Hazen's Brigade and the Ninth Indiana Volunteers. By the time he had recovered sufficiently to return to duty with some restrictions, Hazen's Brigade and the Ninth were marching with Sherman to the sea, and Bierce was unsuccessful in his bid to rejoin them. As if to confirm that something indeed had ended when he parted ways with Hazen, Bierce would write only one war story about the time from his return to duty until war's end.

After moving along the railroad through northern Alabama in October, Bierce participated in the battles of Franklin, Tennessee, in November and Nashville in December. Both cities are on the Tennessee and Alabama railroad line, and the large railhead in Nashville was the terminal. In early January 1865, shortly after the Battle of Nashville, Ambrose Bierce requested a medical discharge from the Union army as a result of lingering problems caused by his head wound. The discharge was granted a few days later.

Bierce wrote three short pieces about this final leg of his wartime journey: the memoir "Four Days in Dixie" already discussed, another entitled "What Occurred at Franklin," and a short story called "The Major's Tale." "The Major's Tale" (1890) has been virtually ignored by critics and is of interest primarily because the action of the story occurs just before Bierce left the service. When Bierce's stories are arranged chronology based on the time of the action in the story, "The Major's Tale" is the final one. The tale itself is little more than an anecdote, a long retrospective account of a practical joke without the typical Biercean macabre twist or snap ending. Although of little literary merit, "The Major's Tale" is one of Bierce's most thoroughly autobiographical war stories and is an appropriate conclusion to his war fiction. Personally as well as from the standpoint of soldierly professionalism, the voice of the narrator in this story gives one a sense of completion by having come full circle.

Characterized as the Confederacy's "last hurrah," the Battle of Nashville was an unsuccessful attempt to lay siege to the Federal garrison that had occupied the city since early 1862. Early in "The Major's Tale," Bierce clearly establishes the time of the action:

> It was a few days before the battle of Nashville. The enemy had driven us up out of northern Georgia and Alabama. At Nashville we had turned at bay and fortified, while old Pap Thomas, our commander, hurried down reinforcements and supplies.
>
> [. . .] I was serving at that time on the staff of a division commander whose name I shall not disclose. [. . .] Our headquarters were in a large dwelling which stood just behind our line of works. (VIII: 65)

While rummaging through the civilian home, some of the staff officers find "an abundant supply of lady-gear—gowns, shawls, bonnets, hats, petticoats and the Lord knows what." The officers concoct an elaborate scheme aimed at Lieutenant Haberton, a staff officer who is "a lady-killer [. . . and] eager that all should know it" (VIII: 66). The staff officers design an elaborate cover story to explain an impending visit by a young southern lady, then dress a smooth-featured Union soldier up as the belle. Haberton, of course, is quickly and easily convinced to be the officer to receive the comely visitor. The officer listens sympathetically while the disguised visitor relates a story of wartime woe and seems to be increasingly anxious about distant Confederate artillery fire. Finally, Haberton is holding both her hands in a gesture of comfort when a shell comes crashing into the house. Unnerved, the imposter jumps up, shouts "Jumping Jee-rusalem!" and begins tearing off his woman's clothing, "exposing his charms in the most shameless way." Haberton, briefly taken aback, attempts a sly grin and announces to gales of laughter, "You can't fool *me*!" (VIII: 75).

As in "Killed at Resaca," the details of the story seem so authentic that there is a great temptation to label it as autobiography. Paul Fatout does exactly that, repeating the story in *The Devil's Lexicographer* as if it were completely factual (57). Once again, the historical context of the story is entirely correct. The narrator's description of the prologue to the battle is accurate, as is the account of the Confederate shelling prior to the battle on December 15 and 16. At the time, Bierce himself was serving as topographic engineer on the staff of General Beatty, a division commander in General Wood's corps. Wood's breastworks were on the south side of Nashville along the Hillsborough and Granny White pikes. Wood made his headquarters "at the elegant residence of Mrs. Acklen, between those highways" (Lossing III: 424). Whether or not Bierce had this mansion or the nearby headquarters of his own division in mind as the setting for "The Major's Tale," his use of an elaborate southern home for a military headquarters is an accurate reflection of Union practices at Nashville.

If the story is autobiographical and Ambrose Bierce is the narrator, then there seems to be a glaring discrepancy: Bierce was a lieutenant, not a major at the time of the Battle of Nashville. This seemingly obvious problem has a relatively simple resolution. The narrator never reveals his rank at the time of the action of the story. The only details he provides about himself are in his statement, "I was serving at that time on the staff of a division commander whose name I shall not disclose, for I am relating facts, and the person upon whom they bear hardest may have surviving relatives who would not care to have him traced" (VIII: 65). With the narrator's introduction of himself, he has also pronounced a license to change names to protect the guilty. Later in the story, the general calls the narrator only by his last name, "Broadwood," with no reference to rank. In other words, the title of the story is ambiguous; it is not clear whether the narrator is a major at the time of the action or the time of the telling. Further, since the narrator announces that he is deliberately obscuring identities, knowing he is called Broadwood in the story does little to help determine his rank.

Most likely, the narrator is a major when he tells the story. He speaks in a deeply retrospective voice. He claims, for example, "You cannot think how young men were in the early sixties! [. . .] Depend on it, my friends, men of that time were greatly younger than men are to-day, but looked much older. The change is quite remarkable. [. . .] And how beautiful the women of those days were!" (VIII: 63–64, 69). The narrator's tone is that of an after-dinner speaker telling an anecdote at a formal reunion many years after the fact. At one point, the narrator even refers to himself as "the harmless skeleton at your feast" (VIII: 72). When Bierce wrote this story, he was in his sixties. It was published in *Negligible Tales*, volume VIII of *The Collected Works*. At the time, Bierce had been living in Washington, DC, for several years and frequented the Army and Navy Club, where he rubbed elbows with the military elite. Here as elsewhere, Bierce was referred to as "Major Bierce." Two years after the war, all Union officers who had served honorably were given an honorary or "brevet" promotion to one rank higher than they held on active duty. Bierce was erroneously brevetted the rank of major instead of captain, an error he never endeavored to correct (Wilt 266). Bierce, then, could very well be the "major" of the tale.

The most intriguing feature of "The Major's Tale" is a brief vignette that is clearly taken from Bierce's life. The final piece in "Bits of Autobiography" is a memoir entitled "A Sole Survivor" (1890). In it, Bierce recalls several events in his life and claims to be the sole survivor of those involved in the event. He then reflects on the responsibilities and the unique position of "sole surviving." The second incident Bierce recalls is a Civil War memory:

> Six men are on horseback on a hill—a general and his staff. Below, in the gray fog of a winter morning, an army, which has left its intrenchments, is moving upon those of the enemy—creeping silently into position. [. . .] the risen sun has burned a way through the fog, splendoring a part of the beleaguered city.
>
> "Look at that, General," says an aide; "it is like enchantment."
>
> "Go and enchant Colonel Post," said the general, without taking his field-glass from his eyes, "and tell him to pitch in as soon as he hears Smith's guns."
>
> All laughed. But to-day I laugh alone. I am the Sole Survivor. (I: 385–86)

Although Bierce does not say where and when it was, the scene he describes is the morning of December 16, 1865, at Nashville. Wiley Sword, in his extremely detailed account of the battle, describes the same morning:

> Sunrise on Friday, December 16, 1864, was shrouded in what one
> observer described as a "Scotch mist." [. . .] by about 8:30 A.M. the
> sun's rays had burned off all but a few lingering patches. [. . .] With
> banners waving and bayonets glistening in the hazy morning sunlight,
> two divisions of A. J. Smith's troops began to advance about 8:00
> A.M. (350–51)

To General A. J. Smith's left was General Wood's Corps, and within
Wood's Corps, Colonel Post was a regimental commander in General
Beatty's division; General Beatty's topographic engineer was Bierce. In
"The Major's Tale," the narrator repeats this same scene on the hillside.
During a digression about the unnamed general, the narrator recalls:

> On that bleak December morning a few days later, when from an hour
> before dawn until ten o'clock we sat on horseback on those icy hills,
> waiting for General Smith to open the battle miles away to the right,
> there were eight of us. At the close of the fighting, there were three.
> There is now one. Bear with him yet a while, oh, thrifty generation;
> he is but one of the horrors of war strayed from his era into yours.
> (VIII: 71–72)

Although of it is no consequence to the plot, Bierce clearly uses a scene
from his own life in the story. Even the deeply retrospective, after-dinner-
speech tone of "A Sole Survivor" is carried into "The Major's Tale." For
all the historical accuracy of the story, it is that tone, the sense of an
event in the distant past and of having come to the end of something,
that gives this, Bierce's final war story about his final battle, an unmis-
takably autobiographical ring. The tale rings so true that it convinces
Fatout the story really did happen and does not leave him wondering if
it did. But one must remember that Bierce can and does increase
verisimilitude by altering names of places and sometimes moving them.
He even announces in this tale that he is going to do the same with the
names of people.

Ultimately, it is another Bierce practice that provides the strongest
piece of evidence that "The Major's Tale" cannot be read as purely autobiographical and that the central event cannot be trusted as fact. When
Bierce edited his *Collected Works*, he placed pieces that he wanted to
present as biographical in the section entitled "Bits of Autobiography."
"The Major's Tale" first appeared as a newspaper column, was then collected in *Can Such Things Be?* along with "Jupiter Doke," "The Mocking-
Bird," "One Kind of Officer," "George Thurston," "The Story of a
Conscience," and a host of ghost and supernatural stories, and finally

appeared, once again with "Jupiter Doke," in the "Negligible Tales" section of *The Collected Works*. In other words, at no time did Bierce ever present "The Major's Tale" as something autobiographical. The placement of it with the clearly fictional "Negligible Tales" especially emphasizes the point. That and the fact that the word *tale* appears in the title augur for best thinking of it as a war story and "truer than anything factual could be."

While neither "The Major's Tale" nor "What Occurred at Franklin" exhibits the sort of gushings bordering on the maudlin that are present in Bierce's West Virginia pieces, the deep-seated nostalgia that emerges in both these end-of-war works is reminiscent of the manner in which Bierce writes of his earliest days in the war. It seems that Bierce frames the beginning and the end of his wartime pilgrimage with sentiment, while filling the middle with the grimmest of storytelling.

Conclusion
The Devil's Topographer

I should be sorry indeed to discredit any of my private animosities by describing them as history.
Ambrose Bierce
in the *San Francisco Examiner*, 7 Oct. 1894

Those who make history do not write it, for they stand too near the event.
William B. Hazen
Preface, *A Narrative of Military Service*

The covers of this book are too far apart.
Bierce
book review

If Bierce's statement from "What I Saw of Shiloh" about incidents grouping themselves "about [his] own personality as a center" serves as a preface to all his Civil War writing, then certainly his description of a topographic engineer's duty at the beginning of "George Thurston" serves as an equally fitting preface to his war stories. After the narrator explains, "It was a business in which the lives of men counted as nothing against the chance of defining a road or sketching a bridge," Bierce makes a revealing point. He tells of a custom in rural England and Wales called "beating the bounds" of the parish. On a certain day, the citizens all turn out and travel to a series of landmarks on parish boundary lines. At each landmark, the village boys are beaten with rods to impress its location on each boy's mind, something that he will need to know as an adult. Bierce claims:

> They become authorities. Our frequent engagements with the Confederate outposts, patrols, and scouting parties had, incidentally, the same educating value; they fixed in my memory a vivid and apparently imperishable picture of the locality—a picture serving instead of accurate field notes, which, indeed it was not always convenient to take, with carbines cracking, sabers clashing, and horses plunging all about. These spirited encounters were observations entered in red. (II: 210–11)

This discussion of beating the bounds does not advance the action of "George Thurston" at all because there is nothing remarkable about any of the "localities" depicted in the story. It is not a tale that depends on any specific or unique terrain feature. But what Bierce does accomplish here is to explain how he is able vividly and accurately to describe places where he had been years before—how even on a very brief mapping expedition, a piece of terrain could become "an apparently imperishable picture." This explanation accomplishes two things. First, because this passage comes at the opening of the first of Bierce's war stories, it serves as the insistence on authenticity, the characteristic "this is no bull" war story tag line, not only for "George Thurston," but for the entire Bierce Civil War canon. Second, it provides an illuminating self-assessment of what Daniel Aaron characterizes as Bierce's "uncanny visual sense" that "managed to fix in his mind the terrain he had traversed" ("Bierce" 172).

When he began publishing war stories, Bierce did not do so with any readily apparent method or predetermined sequence. His earliest publications are not necessarily about events early in the war. Nor did he publish a series or succession of stories that explored a certain theme. When there is a thematically related group of stories, it is their time in the war that puts them in a series, not the time of publication. Nor is there a clear artistic progression over the span of his career as a war story writer. However, if one plots the locations of his stories on (what else but) a map, an accurate chart of Bierce's own progress through the war emerges (maps 1, 4, 12). Almost without exception, not only did Bierce write about the places he knew, but the action of his war stories occurs at times when he was at those places. In stories set at well-known battlefields such as Chickamauga, Stone's River, and Shiloh, one would expect historical and geographical accuracy. However, even in stories such as "A Baffled Ambuscade" and "An Occurrence at Owl Creek Bridge," in which the

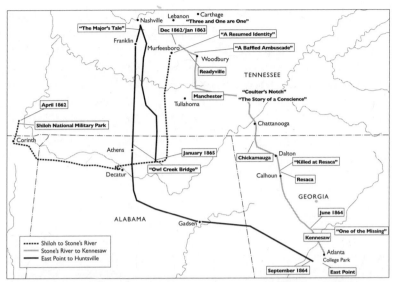

Map 12. The Devil's Topographer. The heavy lines show Bierce's route through the war from Shiloh until his discharge. The small flags show pinpoint locations for selected stories. The general locations of some others are in bold print.

time of the action is far less important because the central events are relatively minor to the course of the war and certainly obscure, Bierce still confines the action at these places to a time when he was there. In so doing, he ensures the accuracy of the larger historical context of his stories. The effect of Bierce's historically correct scenarios is an immediate sense of plausibility, of authenticity, and of unquestioning reader acceptance and complicity in the action of a story as it approaches its inevitably supernatural, psychological, or dramatic conclusion.

Ernest Hemingway included "An Occurrence at Owl Creek Bridge" in his anthology *Men at War: The Best War Stories of All Time.* In characterizing Hemingway's collection, Carlos Baker claims, "Although the volume contained both fiction and nonfiction, Ernest's chief criterion was always verisimilitude" (377). Apparently, Hemingway considered Bierce's tale of Peyton Farquhar "a truer account than anything factual," as it is the lead story in a section of *Men at War* entitled "War Is Fought by Human Beings" (xiv). If the quality of verisimilitude is a criterion for a good war story, then the topographic details of Bierce's settings certainly meet the standard.

Bierce describes terrain with a characteristic topographer's eye for detail. In stories with supernatural elements such as in "A Resumed

Identity" and "A Baffled Ambuscade," Bierce presents the terrain as it exists or existed with little or no fictional modification. In others, such as "The Affair at Coulter's Notch" and "An Occurrence at Owl Creek Bridge," in which events are not supernatural but certainly extraordinary, the general setting is accurate but has elements borrowed from other places Bierce knew and assembled into a fictional montage suited to the tale. Curiously enough, these composite locations add to the stories' believability by obscuring events just enough to make them difficult to confirm with the historical record. Bierce's intimacy with topography is inextricably bound with his service on Hazen's staff. It is virtually impossible to separate the two experiences.

One of the best pieces of scholarship to emerge from an outpouring about Bierce in 1929 was an article in *American Literature* entitled "Ambrose Bierce and the Civil War." In it, Napier Wilt examines Bierce's seven war memoirs in detail and compares them with the archival record and especially with Hazen's *A Narrative of Military Service*. Among Wilt's conclusions is that

> there can be no doubt that Bierce used Hazen's *Narrative* and the *Century* [magazine] articles with intelligence and skill. From them he took a few necessary points of the battles, as few as possible to make the action understandable, and then wrote a clear, swift, vivid, and effective account of the main action. (284)

Although Wilt limits his study strictly to the memoirs, a similar conclusion can be made for much of Bierce's war fiction as well. The imprint of William B. Hazen is unmistakable in the war stories, far more so than has been generally recognized. The number of stories Bierce wrote that have clear connections to his time as Hazen's topographer, thirteen of the twenty-two, indicates that his time with the general was the heart of his service.

Moreover, the table of contents of *A Narrative of Military Service* from the time the Ninth Indiana joined the brigade shortly before Shiloh until the time of Bierce's wounding during the Atlanta campaign reads almost like a catalog of locations for Bierce's war stories and memoirs. For almost every one of Hazen's chapters, there is a corresponding Bierce story and, in several cases, a memoir (fig. 2). These parallels and the fact that Bierce had read *A Narrative of Military Service* by May of 1888, just prior to his prodigious outpouring of war stories from then until 1891, further indicate the importance of Hazen's narrative as a source of Bierce's fiction as well.

CONTENTS.

Fig. 2. Partial table of contents from Hazen's memoir. From *A Narrative of Military Service* (1885; Huntington, WV: Blue Acorn, 1993), vii.

Given that General Hazen once characteristically included in a written operations order the statement "Colonels will be particular to see that every officer is publicly disgraced who leaves his post unnecessarily in action, or fails to exert every effort to execute his duty efficiently" (52), Bierce's thematic concerns with officership, discipline, courage, and duty are additional evidence of his mentor's influence. It is worth noting that this brief statement from Hazen includes aspects of all four of those common Bierce themes. One wonders just how different would have been the life of Ambrose Bierce were it not for his association with William Hazen.

Although there may not be a readily apparent method to the sequence of publication of Bierce's war stories, when one arranges them chronologically by the time of the action, a fairly clear picture of the growth of the artist as a soldier emerges. In his war fiction, there are several concerns that Bierce repeatedly returns to. This study has not examined all of them, but it is clear that when he writes about individual duty in the world of the soldier, he draws on events from 1861; when he writes about issues of military rank, events of 1862; when he writes about issues of officership, 1863; and on the nature of individual courage in staff officers, 1864. Moreover, the later in the war the action of a story is, the more complex or cumulative these themes tend to be. That is to say that a story like "Coulter's Notch" draws on issues of officership that include issues of rank and duty in the world of the soldier. The more experienced Bierce became as a soldier, the more complex the ensuing stories tend to be.

In the end, the discoveries that Bierce habitually writes war stories that are topographically and temporally autobiographical, that he tells ghost war stories on terrain accurately represented, that he obscures the location of other settings by rearranging existing features, that William B. Hazen influenced him even more than generally realized, and that, regardless of when he wrote or published a story, it reflects his development as a soldier more than his development as a writer, both confirm and add additional insight to the work of two prominent Bierce critics. First, they reinforce the picture drawn by Stuart Woodruff of Bierce the fiction writer as a man who, though he would rail at the realists for what he saw as their lack of imagination, was so firmly grounded (perhaps *tethered* is a better word) by his own experiences that he could never quite give full development to his imagination. Second, they reinforce the picture drawn by Morris of Bierce the man who, when all else is "stripped away," remains "1st Lieutenant Ambrose Bierce, Ninth Indiana Infantry, the bloodied veteran" (270). To a degree, Bierce largely confirms this assessment in the 1897 *Examiner* column previously mentioned in connection with "A Son of the Gods." In it Bierce explains that "it commonly occurs that in my poor little battle-yarns the incidents that come in for special reprobation by the critics as 'improbable' and even 'impossible' are transcripts from memory—things that actually occurred before my eyes" (1 Mar 1897).

Afterword
Ambrose Bierce and the American War Story

Prior to the conclusion of the American Civil War there is a dearth of war stories in the canon of American fiction. They are simply not there. Although James Fenimore Cooper and William Gilmore Simms wrote some romances that can arguably be called war novels, they did not publish any short war fiction. The Civil War marks a critical point in the development of the war story in America. War literature during and immediately after the conflict tended to be journalism, speeches, letters, diaries, essays, and memoirs. Due in large part to the magnitude of the war effort and the growth of the newspaper and popular magazine, there was a huge outpouring of this literature, far more than there was following any previous American military operation. The growth of print media sparked a corresponding growth in the popularity of the short story in general and brought the genre to maturity in America. However, it took a big American war to do the same for the war story. In the years following the cessation of hostilities, fictionalized accounts of the conflict began to emerge.

Two exceptional and comprehensive studies of the literature of the Civil War are Edmund Wilson's *Patriotic Gore: Studies in the Literature of the American Civil War* (1962), and Daniel Aaron's *The Unwritten War: American Writers of the Civil War* (1973). In his classic study, Wilson observes, "The period of the American Civil War was not one in which belles lettres flourished" (ix). Aaron expands this notion and accounts for the "literary dearth" by blaming the national "blocking out of race," "the reticence of veterans," the "fastidiousness of lady readers," and "the general rule that national convulsions do not provide the best conditions for artistic creativeness" (xviii). Both authors are commenting on the relatively slow appearance and scarcity of enduring Civil War fiction, yet the phenomenon that Wilson and Aaron describe is not unique to that war. It has happened with every war since.

Aaron's claim citing "the fastidiousness of lady readers" as a reason for the delay in the appearance of war fiction certainly has merit, but it seems a bit too unqualified a statement. While most members of the antebellum novel-reading public were women, there are many counter-examples to Aaron's assertion that "[p]olite literature before and after the War excluded certain kinds of experience, and it is not surprising that the territory of the common soldier should have been placed 'off bounds' by America's cultural guardians. [. . .] The few attempts even to approximate the seamy and unheroic side of the War met with small favor until the next century" (xvii). Polite culture may have hesitated at foregrounding much of the unpleasantness associated with the violence of war, but a couple of brief examples from James Fenimore Cooper should suffice to challenge the notion that it was entirely "off bounds" in nineteenth-century America. This passage appeared in 1826 in *The Last of the Mohicans*:

> The savage spurned the worthless rags [. . .] his bantering but sullen smile changed to a gleam of ferocity, he dashed the head of the infant against a rock, and cast its quivering remains to [its mother's] very feet. [. . .] excited at the sight of blood, the Huron mercifully drove his tomahawk into her own brain. (181)

The following is from *The Deerslayer* in 1841:

> Judith moved forward with a sudden impulse, and removed a canvas cap that was so low on his head as to conceal his face [. . .]. The instant this obstacle was taken away, the quivering and raw flesh, the bared veins and muscles, and all the other disgusting signs of mortality, as they are revealed by tearing away the skin, showed he had been scalped, though still living. (322)

As graphic as these depictions are, and there are many more in Cooper's works, one must wonder just what "certain kinds of experience" Aaron has in mind. It is also somewhat imprecise to claim that realistic war fiction "met with small favor until the next century." In the early 1890s, Bierce's *Tales of Soldiers and Civilians* met with a moderate degree of success, and Stephen Crane's *The Red Badge of Courage* found great public favor starting with its serialized publication in 1894. To hold publishers responsible for the paucity of war literature due to their wishes not to offend simply does not adequately explain the phenomenon.

Aaron suspects another important reason for the long pause between the Civil War and successful war literature is "the blocking out of race."

He conjectures that "One would expect writers [. . .] to say something revealing about the meaning, if not the causes, of the War." It has rarely been the province of American war fiction writers to "say something about the meaning, if not the causes, of the War." Such commentary tends to be the material of nonfiction: histories, essays, sermons, and memoirs of important figures. Wilson also points out that "as soon as a war gets started, few people do any more thinking about anything except demolishing the enemy" (xxxii). Such demolition is the stuff of fiction writers. The enduring fiction writers say something about the meaning, or lack thereof, of battlefield events on soldiers and noncombatants caught in the conflict. Their focus is on causes of individual behavior and examinations of the self in a much-disordered world. Seldom is it analysis of the root causes of national conflict.

Aaron's three closely related observations concerning the "reticence of veterans," "the alleged indifference of the most gifted writers to the War itself," and "the general rule that national convulsions do not provide the best conditions for artistic creativeness" (xviii) also are open to significant counterexamples. Some veterans are reticent to talk openly about their experiences. Others are not. Still others cannot stop talking about them. The extraordinary number of memoirs, diaries, letters, and regimental histories that followed in the wake of the Civil War provides ample evidence that its veterans were not particularly reticent. A more accurate statement might be that veterans seemed reluctant to attempt presenting their experiences as fiction, choosing instead to defer to the literary artists who emerged from their ranks to attempt the daunting task of presenting Hemingway's "truer account than anything factual."

Certainly during the conflict itself, as with most any war, conditions are not best for artistic creativity. Although they may not inspire creativity while combat is ongoing, those same conditions remembered tend to provide plenty of material for literary endeavors after the conflict's end. Aaron's observation about "the best conditions" does not adequately explain the normally long wait from the end of the war to the appearance of enduring fiction. Finally, one must suspect that any "alleged indifference" by gifted writers to producing war fiction might be better explained as simply a reluctance to attempt to capture satisfactorily something they did not personally experience or observe, a point that Edith Wharton makes in her piece of World War I short fiction entitled "Writing a War Story."

What Aaron's observations actually point to is that the "literary dearth" in the wake of the Civil War might simply be a characteristic wait for an artistically gifted participant or observer to emerge. Much of the best fiction concerning subsequent American wars appears at least ten years after their conclusions; it seems that telling "a truer account" takes time, reflection, reconciliation, and a distancing from the immediate calls for patriotic support. Interestingly enough, this literary time-lag pattern established in the aftermath of the Civil War repeats itself in the twentieth century with both world wars and the war in Vietnam. One can explain the dearth of literary war fiction observed by both Wilson and Aaron more easily and credibly with two closely related observations. First, the most enduring war fiction comes from authors who have themselves been combatants or personal observers or had close associations with those who were. Second, authors need sufficient time to digest all they have been through before they can write.

Daniel Aaron's analysis focuses on the reasons for Civil War fiction's failure to appear quickly and in quantity. To understand why the war fiction that eventually did appear was in many ways ahead of its time, it is useful to shift the focus a bit and think of it in terms of why it appeared when it did rather than of when it did not. An explanation of why the best war story writers seem to be aesthetically innovative necessarily involves some speculation; however, a fairly clear pattern emerges. The experience of war for a combatant tends to be an intense and typically disillusioning one. Often it may shatter the combatant's worldview, throwing many of his traditional beliefs about mankind, society, and his country into disarray. That is not to say the same sort of thing does not happen to those who are not directly involved in the conflict, only that the process is greatly accelerated for those who are. Additionally, the combatant will often have experienced depravity and horrors that had been previously foreign to him. If the combatant is also a writer (and survives), he may, as one would expect once he is out of the war, find it extraordinarily difficult to articulate what he has endured. While acknowledging the fact that most writers strive for artistic innovation, it seems reasonable to speculate that one who wants to capture wartime experience may find contemporary craft techniques particularly inadequate for the job. Paul Fussell, describing the British experience in World War I in his landmark study *The Great War and Modern Memory*, states that "finding the war 'indescribable' in any but the available language of traditional literature, those who recalled it had to do so in known literary terms. Joyce, Eliot, Lawrence, Pound, Yeats were not present at the front to induct them into new idioms which might have done the job better" (174). It is not until well after the conflict that authors seem able to innovate beyond "the available language of traditional literature." As Philip Stevick points out, "third-rate minds have always found a way to duplicate easily the prevailing formulas of short fiction" (24). Enduring writers are the ones who innovate, not those who duplicate.

In addition to the delay caused while writers struggle to digest their experiences and describe the indescribable, the appearance and growth of war fiction in the postbellum years was simultaneous with the rise of regionalism in American literature. The increasing urbanization of the country's population, the completion of exploration of the territorial United States, and the growth of the popular magazine have been widely accepted explanations for the growth of local color and regional writing in the years after the war. The regional writers fed a public's growing appetite for realistic depictions of the customs, speech, beliefs, and landscapes of particular areas. In all its basic aspects, war fiction was another type of regionalism. In war fiction the realistic, or at least believable, depictions of the customs, speech, habits, and beliefs of soldiers and others directly affected by combat typically becomes primary material for fictional treatment. War stories offered the opportunity for characters from many regions, often with their attendant and frequently stereotypical regional characteristics, to be thrown together into one of the most truly exotic, curious, and undiscovered regions of all, the battlefield, and to emerge with a new sort of "regional" identity.

Perhaps because, unlike many European nations, the country itself is so vast and diverse, American writers have always been place conscious. Thoreau supplies minute details about the setting of *Walden*; Melville does likewise about the ocean and whaling in *Moby Dick*. And the classic realist and naturalist texts of the last third of the nineteenth century—*A Hazard of New Fortunes*, *Life on the Mississippi*, *The Country of the Pointed Firs*, *Sister Carrie*, and *McTeague*, to name a few—are filled with the specific details of place. In *Hard Facts: Setting and Form in the American Novel*, Philip Fisher claims that American literature has "a small list of privileged settings," and that "[w]hatever actually appears within a society can be interpreted as some variant, some anticipation or displacement or ruin, of one of these privileged settings" (9). Fisher further explains that American literature tends to feature three of these settings: the wilderness, the family farm, and the city. Among war fiction's most frequent concerns are the displacement from and physical ruin of those three settings.

In their introduction to *American Women Regionalists, 1850–1910*, Judith Fetterley and Marjorie Pryse claim, "Regionalist writers frequently connect their interest in character to an interest in development or discovery of identity, specifically in relation to home, region, and community." They further note, "Since the regionalist character tends to develop within her community of origin, her relationship to place—to the regional landscape—is central to her discovery of self" (xvi). It is difficult to find a better example of the discovery of self set in relationship to place than Crane's *The Red Badge of Courage*. Henry Fleming comes from one of Fisher's three privileged settings: the family farm. Forces of war far beyond Fleming's control, however, move him into another of the three settings: the wilderness. But in Fisher's terminology, this is "variant" because it is a wilderness ruined in many respects by war. It is in this rarified and terrible region that Fleming comes to discover, however ironically depicted, "a quiet manhood, nonassertive but of sturdy and strong blood" (139).

Although *The Red Badge of Courage* provides probably the best and most widely recognizable example of the notion of war fiction as a type of regionalism, John William De Forest's *Miss Ravenel's Conversion from Secession to Loyalty* did a similar thing a full twenty-seven years earlier. In addition to its distinction as one of the earliest works of American realism, the novel is also a work of regionalism in two senses. First, it describes in considerable detail the regional worlds of New Haven and New Orleans (twenty-three years before Kate Chopin's first publication). Second, of course, is its accurate presentation of the battlefield as a region. Fisher points out that "[r]egionalism took the first steps towards the deterministic version of experience that we associate with naturalism" because it reflects how the environment of a region shapes its people (122). Like Henry Fleming, *Miss Ravenel's* Edward Colburne is shaped by his war experiences. De Forest exhibits other early glimmerings of naturalism in his war novel; as early as the second paragraph he makes the naturalistic observation that "every great historical event reverberates in a very remarkable manner through the fortunes of a multitude of private and even secluded individuals" (1). Here, as it would do again many times, Civil War fiction anticipated major characteristics of literary trends to come.

Fetterley and Pryse observe that "[a]nother significant feature of regionalist fiction concerns the role of the narrator" (xvii). They claim that, in contrast to the local-colorist narrator who typically appears "superior to and outside of the region of the fiction" (xii), the regionalist "narrator does not distance herself from the inhabitants of the region [. . .] she frequently appears to be an inhabitant herself. [. . .] regional narrators identify with rather than distance themselves from the material of their stories [. . .]" (xvii). This observation helps illuminate why the most enduring war fiction consistently comes from combatants and first-hand observers. For the narrative voice in war fiction to seem distant from the inhabitants of the battlefield, to have the quality of the local colorist, would significantly erode the fundamental quality of verisimilitude. For the voice to appear most convincingly to be an inhabitant, it makes sense that an author who has been there would be most effective. To be told about the region by one with experiential rather than propositional knowledge increases the verisimilitude of the story. Bret Harte headed to the West when he was eighteen, Sara Orne Jewett lived in rural Maine, Kate Chopin in New Orleans, and Mary N. Murfree in the Tennessee hills. All are in the American canon for their writing about what they experienced in those regions. It only stands to reason that war writers would do likewise.

Questions about the necessity of an author being in or observing combat seem reasonable and much akin to questions about the ability of, for example, white authors to write from a black perspective and vice versa or to a woman writer's ability to adopt a man's persona and vice versa. In an introduction to a collection of fifty-six modern war stories, editor Jon E. Lewis points out, "War fiction is, in fact, an unusual sort of fiction: it is invariably fictionalised autobiography" (xv). Lewis himself admits, however, that not every successful author is a combat veteran. A few successful war story authors have never heard a shot fired in anger, yet one cannot ignore Lewis's point about fictionalized autobiography. If one looks to American war fiction for an answer to the must-one-have-been-there-and-done-that question, the evidence overwhelmingly suggests that, beginning with the Civil War, the answer is yes.

Few more well-documented examples exist of the assertion that war fiction "is invariably fictionalized autobiography" than De Forest's 1867 war novel *Miss Ravenel's Conversion from Secession to Loyalty*, the earliest appearance of Civil War fiction that enjoyed any significant degree of literary success. Having published five books by the outbreak of the war, De Forest was already an accomplished author by the time he entered active service for the Union. He recruited a volunteer company in New Haven, Connecticut, and served as a captain from 1862 until he was mustered out at the end of the war. Subsequently De Forest collected many of his wartime letters, memoirs, and journals under the title *A Volunteer's Adventures*, although it was not published until 1946, forty years after his death. *A Volunteer's Adventures* illustrates just how heavily

De Forest drew on his own experiences for material in *Miss Ravenel's Conversion*. As Stanley T. Williams notes, "Parallels between novel and journal are numerous" (vi). Edward Colburne, the protagonist, raises a volunteer company in New Boston, a very thinly disguised version of New Haven. Colburne, being a volunteer and not a regular, is mustered out at war's end just as De Forest was. Miss Ravenel (whom Colburne eventually marries) has a father who is a professor of mineralogy at the Medical College of New Orleans; De Forest's own father-in-law was a geology professor in Charleston. Not only characters from life, but several scenes from *A Volunteer's Adventures* reappear in *Miss Ravenel's Conversion*. In chapter 20 of *Miss Ravenel*, for example, Colburne encounters a series of incidents and wounded soldiers during the battle of Port Hudson, Louisiana, that De Forest describes in his own memoirs of Port Hudson. Not only are the incidents and wounds the same, they happen in an almost identical sequence in the novel as they do in *A Volunteer's Adventures* (*Adventures* 105–10).

Graphic descriptions of battlefield events like the ones just mentioned distinguish *Miss Ravenel's Conversion* as an early example of realism in an American novel. Even R. W. Stallman, Crane's biographer, notes, "Reviewers hailed *The Red Badge of Courage* as the most realistic war novel ever written, and critics since then have claimed that Crane initiated modern realism. But this ignores De Forest" (177). Yet for all its importance as an example of the emerging trend of realism, its merit as the first notable work of fiction to treat war realistically, and its example as work by a soldier-author, *Miss Ravenel's Conversion* is also a flawed novel that will never rank as a first-order classic. The "coincidence of happy marriages" ending, for example, seems right out of many eighteenth- and nineteenth-century romances. Chief among its weaknesses (of which Bierce is also occasionally guilty) is De Forest's use of a very intrusive first-person narrator who is an omniscient observer of the action, yet not a participant in any of it. Most readers find themselves wondering from whom and where this narrative voice comes. In the middle of a battle, for example, the narrator explains, "By the way, I wish the reader to understand that, when I introduce a 'By Jove!' into Van Zandt's conversation, it is to be understood that that very remarkably profane officer and gentleman used the great Name of the True Divinity" (268).

An extremely important breakthrough for Civil War fiction came in 1891 with the publication of Ambrose Bierce's *Tales of Soldiers and Civilians*. Demonstrating the time lag that characterizes most good war story writing, Bierce's first publication of several of the stories in *Tales of*

Soldiers and Civilians had been in newspapers in the late 1880s—over twenty years after the war.

If John William De Forest was the first American fiction writer to treat war realistically and Ambrose Bierce the second, certainly Stephen Crane was the third. Crane appears to be the most prominent exception in American literature to the general rule that the most enduring war fiction comes from authors who have been combatants or firsthand observers. His 1895 novella, *The Red Badge of Courage*, and his 1896 collection of short stories, *The Little Regiment and Other Episodes of the American Civil War*, are classics of the genre and were the first war fiction to meet with widespread public and critical popularity and acclaim. Some critics credit Crane as being the author who "virtually invented modern war fiction" (Lewis xiv), yet Crane was not a participant in the Civil War. He was not born until six years after it was over.

How Crane accomplished the task has been a subject of extensive comment. Most critics overlook the potential significance of Crane's last two years in high school, which he spent at the Hudson River Institute, a military school in Claverack, New York, where he rose to the rank of cadet captain. Crane would later claim that he was at his happiest there. Crane's history professor, the Reverend John Bullock Van Petten, was a major general in the Civil War and frequently reminisced in the classroom about his experiences at Chancellorsville and Antietam. Prior to writing *The Red Badge*, Crane also read extensively about the Civil War and made at least two visits to the battlefields at Chancellorsville (widely recognized as the analogue for the events in *The Red Badge*) and neighboring Fredericksburg. He is also known to have conducted extensive personal interviews with Civil War veterans. Crane found, however, that many of the veterans could not recall details of their sensations during the fighting. Much of that detail is the work of Crane's imagination. As a reviewer reported in 1896, when Crane was asked "where he got his minute knowledge of battle scenes and sensation, he replies that he drew them from his imagination," a technique that stands in obvious contrast to Bierce's battlefield epistemology (qtd. in Stallman 187).

One also wonders if Crane drew some of his "minute knowledge of battle scenes" from Bierce's work. Crane was an unabashed admirer of Bierce. Of "An Occurrence at Owl Creek Bridge," he once allegedly told fellow correspondent and writer Richard Harding Davis that "nothing better exists. That story contains everything" (qtd. in Stallman 264, Stallman and Gilkes, 140). On one or possibly two occasions he wrote in letters to friends, "I deeply admire some short stories by Mr. Bierce"

(*Correspondence* 566).[1] Even a superficial reading reveals similarities between many of the parable-like poems Crane published in 1895 in *The Black Riders* and the satiric short parables Bierce had been publishing in Hearst newspapers. In 1898 Crane published "Death and the Child," a war story in which an innocent child is caught in the gruesome horrors of the battlefield. Bierce had done exactly the same in "Chickamauga" seven years earlier. Although critic Percival Pollard denounced *The Red Badge of Courage* as "an imitation of Bierce" shortly after its appearance (qtd. in Morris 224), and Cathy Davidson probably goes too far when she claims, "Certainly Stephen Crane learned his craft directly from Bierce" (*Experimental* 133), Bierce was clearly an important influence on Crane's war fiction. Ultimately, the student surpassed the teacher and became the better craftsman.

As if to confirm the accuracy of his imagination, Crane, who had been a reporter since 1891, later became a war correspondent and covered both the Greco-Turkish War and the Spanish-American War for Hearst and Pulitzer newspapers. According to Stanley T. Williams, Crane exclaimed in relief when he finally saw battle, "*The Red Badge of Courage* is all right!" (vii). It is also well worth noting that, though Crane is most widely remembered for his Civil War fiction, fully two-thirds of his war fiction concerns the Greco-Turkish and Spanish-American wars. Perhaps because Crane was never a combatant, and clearly his Civil War fiction draws heavily on the experiences of others, most critics overlook the significance of the fact that the bulk of his war fiction comes not from his association with war veterans but from his close personal observations as a war correspondent.

Having examined Bierce's "Killed at Resaca" in a previous chapter, it is worthwhile to return briefly to Fetterley and Pryse's claim that in regionalist fiction, "the narrator does not distance herself from the inhabitants of the region [. . .] she frequently appears to be an inhabitant of the region" (xvii). Bierce's fiction is very consistent with this claim and bolsters the case for reading early Civil War fiction as a type of regionalism.

"Killed at Resaca" and William Dean Howells's war story "Editha" serve as contrasting examples of Fetterley and Pryse's point about narrative distance. The two tales tell very similar stories with very different narrative techniques. Driven by a desire to win glory for themselves vicariously, self-centered young women goad their officer-fiancés to battlefield deaths in both stories. In the end, both women have the opportunity to recognize the error of their self-centered ways yet back away from it.[2]

The author's choice of narrative voice in the two stories is revealing. Howells, of course, is not remembered as a war story writer and purposefully avoided military service by accepting a position as American consul to Venice for the five years of the Civil War. Howells's story is a far more sophisticated psychological study than Bierce's and is reminiscent of some of Henry James's work. Howells tells the story of Editha with a third-person limited narrator. Unlike Bierce's story, "Editha" never takes the reader near the battlefield; the narrative focus remains with Editha and her thoughts throughout. The last the reader and Editha see of her fiancé, George, is when he boards the train with his regiment. The narrator, like Howells, never makes it to the war.

The topographic engineer narrator in "Killed at Resaca" is not only a battlefield observer, he is a participant—a friend and fellow staff officer of the doomed Lieutenant Brayle. There is no distance between the narrator and his subject; they are very much inhabitants of the same region. The narrator even devotes a long paragraph to describing for the reader the "precarious tenure and the unnerving alternation of emotion" that constitute life in combat for staff officers like Brayle and himself (II: 96). De Forest, Bierce, and Crane were instrumental in ushering in this regionalism of the battlefield, a type of regionalism generally quite new to the American reading public.

The era of realism and naturalism, with its artistic links to regionalism, marks the point when American war fiction came of age, and it is difficult to find an author who had a greater influence on the process than Ambrose Bierce. Several features of the war stories of Bierce and Crane stand out as anticipating modernist war fiction to come. Recent critics such as Sean O'Faolain, Frank O'Conner, and Mary Louise Pratt comment on the modern short story's tendency to bring to the center people and experiences who are normally at the fringe of society. O'Conner calls them "submerged population groups" and claims that the success of the modern American short story hinges in large part on "American brutality" and further explains that a "strangeness of behavior which is the very lifeblood of the short story is often an atavistic breaking out from some peculiar way of life, faraway and long ago" (41). Pratt mentions that, in addition to being used for formal experimentation, the short story "is often the genre used to introduce new (and possibly stigmatized) subject matters into the literary arena" (104). It is hard to imagine a type of short fiction more befitting of these comments than Civil War stories. Much of the work of Bierce and Crane views war from the eyes of a hitherto "submerged population group," namely the common soldier. Until then, war fiction had largely consisted of tales of great heroes and captains. With both authors, however, the focus shifted to the private soldier or the junior officer. Certainly this focus combined with the unflinching treatment of battlefield grotesques and the "strangeness of behavior" that combat is likely to produce introduced new and previously "improper" material to the American short story well before the modern short story began doing so with other population groups.

"An Occurrence at Owl Creek Bridge" alone exhibits several salient features of modernism and even postmodernism. It is experimental: the bulk of the story consists of elaborate flashbacks and flash-forwards in the doomed protagonist's mind. The workings of his mind trick not only him but the reader as well. It is quite concerned with consciousness and with the unconscious: in addition to the flashing forward, the reader encounters the protagonist's extremely distorted sensory input and must depend on it. Consequently, the reader draws a lesson in the limitations of perception. It begins *in medias res*, a point that carries a bit more significance than it might initially appear. O'Faolain claims that a hallmark of the modern short story is its characteristic disregard for opening conventions such as "Once upon a time" (or perhaps "This is no bull!"). O'Faolain further explains that modern writers "showed readers that if they were [. . .] 'quick on the uptake' they could dive into the narrative" without contrived conventions aimed at establishing verisimilitude by suspending disbelief (150). Certainly it is difficult to imagine a more in-the-middle-of-things opening than Bierce's in "Owl Creek Bridge":

> A man stood on a railroad bridge in northern Alabama, looking down into the swift water twenty feet below. The man's hands were behind his back, the wrists bound with a cord. A rope closely encircled his neck. (II: 27)

Such innovations in Bierce's fiction lead Brigid Brophy to suggest, with tongue in cheek, that magic realist Jorge Luis Borges is really Bierce writing under a nom de plume (qtd. in Davidson, *Experimental* 5). Davidson agrees and argues that "Bierce more than any other nineteenth-century American writer anticipates the revolutions in ideas of art and life that characterize the innovative and experimental fictions of the present era" (*Experimental* 123).

One aspect of Stephen Crane's war fiction that places it at the forefront of literary development is his use of imagery. Crane's work anticipates much of what was to come in the imagist movement formalized by Ezra Pound, Amy Lowell, H.D., and others. In *Stephen Crane and Literary Impressionism*, James Nagel convincingly establishes the influence of impressionist painting on Crane's literary work. Whereas realism endeavors to present things as they are, impressionism seeks to represent things as they appear to human senses at a particular time. Often, this sensory input may be distorted by obscurants such as smoke, fog, darkness, windows, walls, and other impediments. As a result, the perceiver may not accurately interpret sensory input because his perception is incomplete. As one might expect, such a presentation draws heavily on the use of images, particularly visual ones. *The Red Badge* is extremely rich in such imagery. The most prominent example is at the end of chapter 9 when, after witnessing the agonized death of his friend Jim Conklin, Henry Fleming

> turned, with sudden, livid rage toward the battlefield. He shook his fist. He seemed about to deliver a philippic.
> "Hell—"
> The red sun was pasted in the sky like a wafer. (62)

Assuming that the wafer is red wax of the type used to seal letters in Crane's day, the image memorably captures all of Henry's rage and frustration at the event he has just witnessed. A more heavy-handed use of the same technique occurs at the end of the novel. In a moment of peaceful reverie after the battle, Fleming's thoughts turn

> to images of tranquil skies, fresh meadows, cool brooks—an existence of soft and eternal peace.
> Over the river a golden ray of sun came through the hosts of leaden rain clouds. (140)

As Nagel points out, moments such as these serve as excellent examples of Pound's definition of an image as a device that "presents an intellectual and emotional complex in an instant of time" (qtd. in Nagel 29). Certainly these examples also illustrate the first two tenets of Pound's imagist manifesto, namely "direct treatment of the 'thing,' whether subjective or objective," and "to use absolutely no word that does not contribute to the presentation" (147). Even Carl Sandburg acknowledges a debt to Crane when he writes to "Stevie Crane" in "Letters to Dead Imagists." Sandburg, playing on Crane's poem "War Is Kind," states that "War is kind and we never knew the kindness of war till you came" (qtd. in Nagel 174). Nagel goes so far as to claim:

> The relativistic realities of Crane's Impressionism play a key role in the development of what came to be know as Modernism, especially in its sense of an indifferent and undefinable universe. [. . .] His evocative and surrealistic imagery predicts similar strategies in Expressionism. [. . .]

the interpretive uncertainties of his Impressionism foreshadow the absurdity of the French New Novel and much of Post-Modernism. (174–75)

It is somewhat remarkable that critics as distinguished and diverse as Davidson and Nagel find clearly such postmodern qualities in Civil War fiction.

An aspect of Tim O'Brien's *The Things They Carried* that distinguishes it as an important work of postmodernism is the author's blurring of the line between fiction and autobiography. The work is not a traditional novel, nor is it a short story cycle in the traditional sense. Throughout, the narrative voice is a middle-aged war veteran named Tim who was an infantryman and is now a writer. Many readers immediately assume the narrator is the autobiographical voice of the author. Clearly, O'Brien bases much of the book on his experiences, yet he also never presents events as wholly factual. Most readers of *The Things They Carried* find themselves asking, at some point, the same question as Bierce readers: "I wonder if that really happened?" In stories such as "Killed at Resaca," "George Thurston," and "The Major's Tale," Ambrose Bierce was doing essentially the same thing for which Tim O'Brien would win praise one hundred years later.

When Walt Whitman claimed that "the real war will never get into the books," he was echoing a sentiment expressed by Frederick L. Olmstead, who, in a letter to his wife in June of 1862, wrote, "The horror of war can never be known but on the field. It is beyond, far beyond all imagination" (qtd. in Aaron, *Unwritten War* 152). In attempting to find adequate means to stretch readers' imaginations and bring the horror from field to printed page, Whitman and others produced work that anticipated future trends. The Civil War fiction of John William De Forest was clearly exhibiting features of realism before it became a well-established literary movement. De Forest, along with Ambrose Bierce and Stephen Crane, also helped to usher in a different sort of regionalism, that of the battlefield, which was a precursor of much naturalistic fiction. Modernist qualities emerge in much of Bierce's war fiction, and Crane's impressionistic work anticipates the Imagists. These three American authors, all participants in or firsthand observers of war, were marching a step ahead of the literary pack. If the era of realism and naturalism marks the point when American war fiction came of age, certainly the era of modernism marks its coming to full maturity, for De Forest, Bierce, and Crane were strong influences on Hemingway, Dos Passos, Salinger, O'Brien, and other twentieth-century authors of war fiction.

Appendix 1

Bierce's Civil War Stories in Chronology

Story title	Time of story	Location of story	Date Bierce at location or location of Bierce at time	First published
A Tough Tussle	Autumn 1861	West Virginia		Sept. 1888
The Mockingbird	Autumn 1861	West Virginia	Jun.–Dec. 1861	May 1891
A Horseman in the Sky	Autumn 1861	West Virginia	Jun.–Dec. 1861	April 1889
Two Military Executions	Spring 1862	Shiloh, TN	April 1862	Nov. 1906
The Coup de Grâce	1862	Shiloh, TN	April 1862	June 1889
An Affair of Outposts	Spring 1862	Near Shiloh	Apr.–Jun. 1862	Dec. 1897
An Occurrence at Owl Creek Bridge	Summer 1862	Northern AL	Jun. '62, late '64, Jan. '65–Jun. '66	July 1890
A Resumed Identity	Dec 1862	Murfreesboro, TN	Dec. 1862–Mar. 1863	Sept. 1908
A Baffled Ambuscade	Early 1863 and many years later	Readyville & Woodbury, TN	Early 1863; revisits in 1907	Nov. 1906
The Story of a Conscience	Autumn 1861 and summer 1863?	Grafton, WV, & Cumberlands	Grafton: 1861; Cumberlands: 1863	June 1890

Continued on next page

Story title	Time of story	Location of story	Date Bierce at location or location of Bierce at time	First published
Parker Adderson, Philosopher	?	?		Feb. 1891
The Affair at Coulter's Notch	Summer 1863	Tennessee	Summer 1863	Oct. 1889
One Kind of Officer	?	?		Jan. 1893
Three and One Are One	Late summer 1863	Carthage, TN	Summer 1863	Oct. 1908
One Officer, One Man	1863	?	Tennessee	Feb. 1889
Chickamauga	Sept. 1863	Chickamauga, GA	Sept. 1863	Jan. 1889
Jupiter Doke	Nov. 1861– Feb. 1862	"Distilleryville, KY"	Oct. 1864, Wauhatchie, TN	Dec. 1885
Killed at Resaca	May 1864	Resaca, GA	May 1864	June 1887
A Son of the Gods	?	?		July 1888
George Thurston	1863 or later (fall 1864?)	?	In TN, AL, & GA ('63–'65)	Sept. 1883
One of the Missing	June 1864	Kennesaw, GA	June 1864	March 1888
The Major's Tale	Dec. 1864	Nashville, TN	Dec. 1864	Jan. 1890

Question mark indicates that the time and/or location cannot be determined.

Appendix 2

Bierce's Civil War Time Line and Related Stories

Chronology		Related Stories
1861		
Apr. 25	9th Indiana musters	
June 1	Arrives at Grafton, WV	
June 3	Battle of Philippi	
July 10	Battle of Laurel Hill	
July 14	Battle of Carrick's Ford	
July–Aug.	9th remusters as 3-yr. reg., returns to Grafton, WV	
Aug. 14	Bierce promoted to sergeant	
Sept. 5	Promoted to first sergeant	
Oct. 3	Battle of Greenbrier	Mentioned in "The Story of A Conscience"
Dec. 13	Attack on Camp	"A Tough Tussle" (1888)
	Allegheny	"A Horseman in the Sky" (1889)
		"The Mocking-Bird" (1891)
1862		
Feb. 19	9th assigned to Buell's Army of the Ohio	"Jupiter Doke, Brigadier-General" (1885) (see also Oct. 27, 1863)
Mar. 2	9th arrives at Nashville, assigned to Hazen's Brigade	
Apr. 6, 7	Battle of Shiloh	mentioned in "The Mocking-Bird"
		mentioned in "An Affair of Outposts" (1897)
		"Two Military Executions" (1906)
		"The Coup de Grace" (1889)

Continued on next page

May 30	Fall of Corinth	mentioned in "Owl Creek Bridge"
June	Railroad repair	"An Occurrence at Owl Creek Bridge" (1890)
Dec. 1	Bierce commissioned as second lieutenant	"A Resumed Identity" (1908)
Dec. 30, 31	Battle of Stone's River (site revisited by Bierce 1907)	

<u>1863</u>

Mar.	Bierce assigned to brigade headquarters as provost marshal	
Apr.	Becomes topographic engineer; Readyville	"A Baffled Ambuscade" (1906)
Apr. 25	Promoted to first lieutenant	
Apr.	Hazen's Brigade assigned to Rosecrans's Army of the Cumberland Tullahoma campaign	"The Story of a Conscience" (1890) "Parker Adderson" (1891) [?] "Coulter's Notch" (1889) "One Kind of Officer" (1893) [?] "Three and One Are One" (1908)
Sept. 19, 20	Battle of Chickamauga	"One Officer, One Man" (1889) "Chickamauga" (1889)
Oct. 27	Charge of the mules	Analogue for "Jupiter Doke"
Nov. 24, 25	Battle of Missionary Ridge	Mentioned in "One of the Missing"
Dec. 12	9th on furlough	

<u>1864</u>

Feb.	9th returns to duty	
May 15	Battle of Resaca	"Killed at Resaca" (1887) "A Son of the Gods" (1888) [?]
May 27	Pickett's Mill	
June 23	Bierce wounded at Kennesaw Mtn.	"One of the Missing" (1888)
Late Sept.	Returns to duty with Post's Brigade	"George Thurston" (1883) [?]
Oct.	Briefly captured by Confederates	
Nov. 28–30	Battle of Franklin	"The Major's Tale" (1890)
Dec. 15, 16	Battle of Nashville	

Notes

Introduction

1. One of Schaefer's most important secondary sources is John Keegan's classic study of behavior in combat, *The Face of Battle*, a book that also richly informs this entire project. As one reviewer very accurately observed, "It would be a pity if this book were labelled 'military history' and read only by military historians. It raises issues that concern anyone who takes an interest in the fate of his children."

2. Duncan and Klooster's *Phantoms of a Blood-Stained Period: The Complete Civil War Writings of Ambrose Bierce* is an extremely helpful anthology that, for the first time, brings together Bierce's Civil War fiction, memoirs, poetry, letters, newspaper columns, and even a couple of maps under one cover. It was published while this book was undergoing manuscript revisions and would have saved this author many, many research hours. Duncan and Klooster group Bierce's writings chronologically by war year. Their temporal placement of stories is, with only a few exceptions, very consistent with this book's.

3. Unless otherwise noted, parenthetical citations of Bierce's work are from *The Collected Works of Ambrose Bierce*, volumes I–XII. The volume number appears in Roman numerals followed by the page number. While other collections of Bierce's Civil War stories are more readily available, *The Collected Works* is the last publication Bierce had a personal hand in and is the most authoritative. The Gordian Press made access to copies of the collection far easier when, in 1966, it published facsimile editions of the original.

Chapter I

1. References to the United States Department of War's *The War of the Rebellion: A Compilation of the Official Records of the Union and Confederate Armies* will be parenthetically cited as *OR* followed by the series number, volume number in Roman numeral, and page number.

2. A book that, fortunately, was brought back into print in 1993 by the Blue Acorn Press.

Chapter 2

1. In 1904, Bierce also wrote a memoir-like letter for inclusion in the Ninth Indiana Veteran Volunteer Infantry Association's eighteenth annual reunion proceedings. The letter was reprinted as *Battlefields and Ghosts* in 1931. Its tone echoes much of what is found in the two memoirs discussed. The twelfth and final volume of *The Collected Works*, *In Motley*, contains a hodgepodge of sketches, satiric short plays, essays, and a few short stories. Because Bierce entitled Volume XI *Antepenultima*, one wonders if he had plans for a thirteenth volume that never materialized.

2. Remarkably, Traveler's Repose, the post office and inn by the Greenbrier River that Bierce mentions in "A Bivouac of the Dead" is still intact. It is a well-kept private dwelling occupied at the time of this writing by the elderly niece of the postmaster-innkeeper Bierce describes in the memoir. Although vandals have stolen most of the homemade grave markers, the Confederate graves on the hillside behind the old inn are largely as Bierce describes them and still contrast starkly with the perfectly manicured Union gravesites at the old Grafton National Cemetery.

3. Bierce recast the essential action of "A Tough Tussle" in a civilian setting again in the *San Francisco Examiner* less than two years later when he published "The Man and the Snake." In "The Man and the Snake," Harker Brayton, a guest in the mansion-like home of a prominent zoologist specializing in reptiles, finds himself alone in his room late at night confronting what he thinks is a species of cobra escaped from the zoologist's "snakery" also located in the mansion. Brayton, who initially scoffs at tales of the snake's ability to hypnotize its victims, finds himself staring at the creature across the room under a dresser. The snake is Brayton's own bête noire, and he finds himself coming under the serpent's control. Violently convulsing, he eventually dies of fright under the spell of what turns out to be a stuffed snake with shoe-button eyes. As in "A Tough Tussle," the protagonist finds himself confronting a primal fear, largely in darkness, becoming completely unnerved by the extraordinary psychological experience, and dying as a result.

4. The story of William Sites and the story of the rattlesnake den appeared on a temporary display board at the Seneca Rocks Visitors' Center in the summer of 1997. The exhibit has since been replaced.

5. In his classic study of British writing about World War I, *The Great War and Modern Memory*, Paul Fussell makes much of the fact that British soldiers of the war frequently identified themselves with Bunyan's pilgrim. As he does with regard to several of Fussell's other salient points, Bierce anticipates World War I writers.

Chapter 3

1. In *The Devil's Dictionary*, Bierce defines *misericorde* as "a dagger which in mediaeval warfare was used by the foot soldier to remind the unhorsed

knight that he was mortal" (VII: 219). The weapon was typically used for mercy killing.

2. Technically, Grant was not relieved of command. He was reduced to second in command of the army. President Lincoln loyally supported Grant and made the oft-quoted statement, "I can't spare this man; he fights" in the general's defense (qtd. in U.S. Army Center 215).

3. Critics have long been divided over the story. Some characterize it as a classic example of the story with a trick or snap ending, typically admitting that the tale is wonderfully well crafted but, like all Bierce's work, lacking in artistic merit or original psychological insight. Others regards it as an example of a story that masterfully draws readers into unquestioning acceptance of the protagonist's distorted sensory input with the larger point being a sobering lesson about trusting one's own perceptions and reasoning. Lawrence I. Berkove's recent *A Prescription for Adversity: The Moral Art of Ambrose Bierce* is in the latter category. His analysis of "Owl Creek Bridge" is a brilliant apologia. He makes a very compelling case for his reading of the protagonist as an unheroic man whose emotions overtake his reason, and all the while the same thing is happening to the reader, who becomes fully complicit in the fantasy. The tale is a literary hoax of the highest order claims Berkove.

4. The version quoted here is from a newspaper clipping in a Bierce scrapbook that served as the manuscript for *Tales of Soldiers and Civilians* and is part of the University of Virginia's collection. Bierce's own heavy pencil editing appears throughout these newspaper versions that he pasted in his scrapbooks. Unfortunately, what newspaper the clipping is from cannot be determined, as no publication data accompanies it. Most likely, it is from the *San Francisco Examiner*, which first published the story about a year and a half before the appearance of *Tales of Soldiers and Civilians*.

5. Information in this paragraph is from the author's personal observations along the route of the railroad and from Van Horne, pages 163–66 and 439–58.

Chapter 4

1. See also chapter 1, page 10.

2. The lieutenant's shocking vision of himself in the pool of water may seem, to some, a Biercean twist on Eve's seeing her reflection in Milton's *Paradise Lost*. This is certainly a possibility, as Bierce knew Milton's work. In *The Devil's Dictionary* under the definition of *gunpowder*, he notes that "Milton says it was invented by the devil to dispel angels with, and this opinion seems to derive some support from the scarcity of angels" (VII: 125). In the "Epigrams" section to *Negligible Tales*, Bierce quips, "When Eve first saw her reflection in a pool, she sought Adam and accused him of infidelity" (VIII: 365).

3. The story was made into a film with the help of a generous grant from the National Endowment for the Humanities, which funded a project that turned nine American short stories into a film series entitled *The American Short Story.*
4. In "An Affair of Outposts" the word *affair* has the same function.
5. For information on the families of Chickamauga, see Tucker 376–77; also very helpful is Cozzens 418.
6. For information on Eliza Glenn and her family, see Cozzens 139–40, Tucker 139, and Hollister 16.
7. Although "Jupiter Doke" was his only epistolary war story, Bierce wrote at least two others, "The Failure of Hope & Wandel" and "Why I Am Not Editing 'The Stinger,'" using the convention. Both are in volume VIII of *The Collected Works.*
8. Another bit of punning with names—Dod Grile = doggerel.
9. Information in this paragraph is compiled from Hazen 156–65, Long 427, and Morris 67–68.
10. Hazen devotes an inordinate number of pages in his narrative to defending a claim that his troops, not those of General Philip Sheridan, got there first. It was an argument both generals would carry on long after the war's end.

Chapter 5

1. Readers may notice affinities between "Killed at Resaca" and William Dean Howell's "Editha," published in 1905. The point will be more fully discussed in the Afterword.
2. Additional confirmation that there is not a gully near Hazen's positions was made with the U.S. Geologic Survey's 1: 24,000-scale topographic map of the area and a personal visit to the site of Bierce's map of Resaca.
3. Information on the Battle of Kennesaw Mountain was compiled from Hazen 263–65, Scaife 40–47, and Yates 11–23.

Afterword

1. Thanks to Michael W. Schaefer for pointing out that only one Crane letter saying he deeply admired Bierce's short stories can be authenticated. Thomas Beer, an early Crane biographer, cites a similar letter, but he appears to have forged what he claimed to be Crane correspondence.
2. Whether or not "Killed at Resaca" influenced Howells is impossible to say, though the similarities are remarkable. Howells complimented Bierce's work on public occasions, but the two never met. Bierce frequently lambasted Howells and the eastern literary establishment in newspaper columns; the only area where he seemed in agreement with Howells was his opposition to the Spanish-American War.

Bibliography

Aaron, Daniel. "Ambrose Bierce and the American Civil War." *Uses of Literature*. Ed. Monroe Engel. Cambridge: Harvard University Press, 1973. Rpt. in *Critical Essays on Ambrose Bierce*. Ed. Cathy N. Davidson. Boston: Hall, 1982. 169–81.

———. *The Unwritten War: American Writers and the Civil War*. New York: Knopf, 1973.

Ames, Clifford R. "Do I Wake or Sleep? Technique as Content in Ambrose Bierce's Short Story, 'An Occurrence at Owl Creek Bridge.'" *American Literary Realism* 19 (1987): 52–67.

"An Act of Justice." *Elkhart Review*. 28 Feb. 1863.

Armstrong, Zella. *The History of Hamilton County and Chattanooga, Tennessee*. Chattanooga: Lookout, 1931.

Baker, Carlos. *Ernest Hemingway: A Life Story*. 1969. New York: Collier, 1988.

Baumgartner, Richard A. Introduction. Hazen, *Narrative* v–xxiv.

Bhagavad-Gita. Trans. Barbara Stoler Miller. New York: Bantam, 1986.

Bierce, Albert. Letter to Ambrose Bierce. 27 March 1911. Papers of Ambrose Bierce. University of Virginia Lib., Charlottesville, VA.

Bierce, Ambrose. *Ambrose Bierce's Civil War*. Ed. William McCann. Washington, DC: Regnery Gateway, 1956.

———. *Battlefields and Ghosts*. Palo Alto: Harvest, 1931.

———. *The Civil War Short Stories of Ambrose Bierce*. Ed. Ernest J. Hopkins. Lincoln: University of Nebraska Press, 1988.

———. *The Collected Works of Ambrose Bierce*. 12 vols. 1909–12. New York: Gordian, 1966.

———. *The Letters of Ambrose Bierce*. Ed. Bertha Clark Pope. 1922. New York: Gordian, 1967.

———. *A Much Misunderstood Man: Selected Letter of Ambrose Bierce*. Ed. S. T. Joshi and David E. Schultz. Columbus: Ohio State University Press, 2003.

———. The Papers of Ambrose Bierce, a.n. 5992. University of Virginia Lib., Charlottesville, VA.

———. *Phantoms of a Blood-Stained Period: The Complete Civil War Writings of Ambrose Bierce*. Ed. Russell Duncan and David J. Klooster. Amherst: University of Massachusetts Press, 2002.

Black, Robert C. *The Railroads of the Confederacy.* Chapel Hill: University of North Carolina Press, 1952.

Brandt, Robert. *Touring the Middle Tennessee Backroads.* Winston-Salem, NC: Blair, 1995.

Berkove, Lawrence I. *A Prescription for Adversity: The Moral Art of Ambrose Bierce.* Columbus: Ohio State University Press, 2002.

Bunyan, John. *The Pilgrim's Progress.* 1688. Rpt. as *Grace Abounding and The Pilgrim's Progress.* Cambridge: Cambridge University Press, 1907.

Burney, Saffold. *Hand-Book of Alabama.* Birmingham, AL: Roberts, 1892.

Catton, Bruce. *The Coming Fury.* 1961. New York: Pocket Books, 1967.

———. *This Hallowed Ground.* 1956. New York: Pocket Books, 1961.

———. *Never Call Retreat.* 1965. New York: Pocket Books, 1967.

———. *Terrible Swift Sword.* 1963. New York: Pocket Books, 1967.

Cheatham, George, and Judy Cheatham. "Bierce's 'An Occurrence at Owl Creek Bridge.'" *Explicator* 43 (1984): 45–46.

"A Complaint." *Elkhart Review.* 20 Dec. 1862.

Cooper, James Fenimore. *The Deerslayer.* New York: Bantam Books, 1982.

———. *The Last of the Mohicans.* New York: Bantam Books, 1981.

Couser, Thomas G. "Writing the Civil War: Ambrose Bierce's 'Jupiter Doke, Brigadier-General.'" *Studies in American Fiction* 18 (Spring 1990): 87–98.

Cozzens, Peter. *This Terrible Sound: The Battle of Chickamauga.* Urbana: University of Illinois Press, 1992.

Crane, Stephen. *The Black Riders and Other Lines.* Boston: Copeland and Day, 1895.

———. *The Correspondence of Stephen Crane.* Ed. Stanley Wertheim and Paul Sorrentino. New York: Columbia University Press, 1988.

———. *The Red Badge of Courage.* 1895. New York: Bobbs-Merrill, 1964.

Davidson, Cathy N. Introduction. *Critical Essays on Ambrose Bierce.* Boston: Hall, 1982.

———. *The Experimental Fictions of Ambrose Bierce: Structuring the Ineffable.* Lincoln: University of Nebraska Press, 1984.

De Forest, John William. *Miss Ravenel's Conversion From Secession to Loyalty.* 1867. New York: Rinehart, 1955.

———. *A Volunteer's Adventures: A Union Captain's Record of the Civil War.* New Haven: Yale University Press, 1946.

Fatout, Paul. "Ambrose Bierce (1841–1914)." *American Literary Realism* 1 (1967): 13–19.

———. "Ambrose Bierce, Civil War Topographer." *American Literature* 26 (1954): 391–400.

———. *Ambrose Bierce: The Devil's Lexicographer.* Norman: University of Oklahoma Press, 1951.

Fetterley, Judith, and Marjorie Pryse, eds. *American Women Regionalists, 1850–1910.* New York: Norton, 1992.

Fisher, Philip. *Hard Facts: Setting and Form in the American Novel.* New York: Oxford University Press, 1985.

Fitch, John. *Annals of the Army of the Cumberland.* Philadelphia: Lippincott, 1864.

Fitch, Michael Hendrick. *The Chattanooga Campaign.* Madison: Wisconsin State History Commission, 1911.

Forrest, Nathan B. *Abstract of Manuscript Order Book of General Forrest's Cavalry Corps, C.S.A.* Ts. 133497. U.S. Military Academy Library, West Point, NY.

Foster, Thomas C. *How to Read Literature like a Professor: A Lively and Entertaining Guide to Reading between the Lines.* New York: Quill, 2003.

Foulke, William D. *Life of Oliver P. Morton, Including His Important Speeches.* 2 vols. Indianapolis: Bowen-Merrill, 1899.

Freiburg, Herder. *The Herder Symbol Dictionary.* Trans. Boris Matthews. Wilmette, IL: Chiron, 1986.

Fussell, Paul. *The Great War and Modern Memory.* London: Oxford University Press, 1975.

The Goodspeed Histories of Cannon, Coffee, DeKalb, Warren and White Counties. 1887. McMinnville, TN: Lomond, 1972.

Grattan, C. Hartley. *Bitter Bierce: A Mystery of American Letters.* Garden City, NY: Doubleday, 1929.

Grenander, Mary E. *Ambrose Bierce.* New York: Twayne, 1971.

Hackworth, David H. *About Face: The Odyssey of an American Warrior.* New York: Simon, 1989.

Hazen, William B. *A Narrative of Military Service.* 1885. Huntington, WV: Blue Acorn, 1993.

———. Letter to Ambrose Bierce. 3 December 1885. Papers of Ambrose Bierce. University of Virginia Lib., Charlottesville, VA.

———. Letter to Commissioner of Pensions. Hand copy dated 20 December 1887 of 1886 original. Papers of Ambrose Bierce. University of Virginia Lib., Charlottesville, VA.

———. Letter to Headquarters, Military District of Atlanta. 30 Sep 1864. Papers of Ambrose Bierce. University of Virginia Lib., Charlottesville, VA.

Hemingway, Ernest. *Ernest Hemingway: Selected Letters.* Ed. Carlos Baker. New York: Scribner's, 1981.

———. Introduction. *Men at War: The Best War Stories of All Time.* New York: Bramhall, 1942.

Hewett, Janet, ed. *Supplement to the Official Records of the Union and Confederate Armies.* Pt. II, vol. 22, ser. 34. Wilmington, NC: Broadfoot, 1996.

Hollister, John J. *Chickamauga and Chattanooga on Your Own: An Illustrated Guide to the Battlefields.* Chattanooga: Battlefield Guide, 1977.

Hopkins, Ernest J. Foreword. *The Civil War Short Stories of Ambrose Bierce.* By Ambrose Bierce. Lincoln: University of Nebraska Press, 1970.

Joshi, S. T. and David E. Schultz. *Ambrose Bierce: An Annotated Bibliography of Primary Sources.* Westport, CN: Greenwood, 1999.

Kalter, Susan. "'Chickamauga' as an Indian-Wars Narrative: The Relevance of Ambrose Bierce for a First-Nations-Centered Study of the Nineteenth Century." *Arizona Quarterly* 56 (Winter 2000): 57–82.

Keegan, John. *The Face of Battle.* New York: Viking, 1976.

Lewis, Jon E. Introduction. *War: A Classic Collection of 56 Great War Stories of Our Time.* New York: Galahad, 1993.

Long, E. B. *The Civil War Day by Day: An Almanac, 1861–1865.* Garden City, NY: Doubleday, 1971.

Lossing, Benson J. *Pictorial History of the Civil War in the United States of America.* 3 vols. Hartford: Belknap, 1866–68.

Mariani, Giorgio. "Ambrose Bierce's Civil War Stories and the Critique of the Martial Spirit." *Studies in American Fiction* 19 (Autumn 1991): 221–28.

McCann, William. Introduction. *Ambrose Bierce's Civil War.* 1956. Washington, DC: Regnery Gateway, 1991.

McElfresh, Earl B. *Maps and Mapmakers of the Civil War.* New York: Abrams, 1999.

McWilliams, Carey. *Ambrose Bierce: A Biography.* New York: Albert Boni, 1929.

Medley, Landon Daryle. *The History of Van Buren County, Tennessee: The Early Canebreakers, 1840–1940.* Salem, WV: Mills, 1987.

Mencken, H. L. "Ambrose Bierce." *Prejudices: Sixth Series.* New York: Knopf, 1927. Rpt. in *Critical Essays on Ambrose Bierce.* Ed. Cathy N. Davidson. Boston: Hall, 1982. 61–64.

Merrill, Catherine. *The Soldier of Indiana in the War for the Union.* 2 vols. Indianapolis: Merrill, 1866, 1869.

Morris, Roy, Jr. *Ambrose Bierce: Alone in Bad Company.* New York: Crown, 1995.

Morrow, William. Letter to Ambrose Bierce. 10 July 1886. Papers of Ambrose Bierce. University of Virginia Lib., Charlottesville, VA.

Nagel, James. *Stephen Crane and Literary Impressionism.* University Park: Pennsylvania State University Press, 1980.

O'Brien, Matthew C. "Ambrose Bierce and the Civil War: 1865." *American Literature* 48 (1976): 377–81.

O'Brien, Tim. *The Things They Carried: A Work of Fiction.* Boston: Houghton, 1990.

O'Conner, Frank. *The Lonely Voice: A Study of the Short Story.* 1963. New York: Harper, 1985.

O'Conner, Richard J. *Ambrose Bierce: A Biography.* Boston: Little, 1967.

O'Faolain, Sean. *The Short Story.* New York: Devin-Adair, 1951.

Olderr, Steven. *Symbolism: A Comprehensive Dictionary.* Jefferson, NC: McFarland, 1986.

Owens, David M. "Bierce and Biography: The Location of Owl Creek Bridge." *American Literary Realism* 26 (Spring 1994): 82–89.

Plato. "Apology." In *The Trial and Death of Socrates.* Trans. G. M. A. Grube. Indianapolis: Hackett, 1975.

Pope, Bertha Clark. Introduction. *The Letters of Ambrose Bierce.* 1922. New York: Gordian, 1967.

Pound, Ezra. "Vorticism." *The Modern Tradition: Backgrounds of Modern Literature.* Ed. Richard Ellmann and Charles Feidelson, Jr. Oxford: Oxford University Press, 1965. 145–52.

Pratt, Mary Louise. "The Short Story: The Long and Short of It." *Poetics* 10 (1981). Rpt. in *The New Short Story Theories.* Ed. Charles E. May. Athens: Ohio University Press, 1994. 91–112.

Randall, James G., and David Herbert Donald. *The Civil War and Reconstruction.* 2nd ed. Lexington, MA: Heath, 1969.

Saunders, Richard. *Ambrose Bierce: The Making of a Misanthrope.* San Francisco: Chronicle, 1985.

Scaife, William R. *The Campaign for Atlanta.* Atlanta: William R. Scaife, 1985.

Schaefer, Michael W. *Just What War Is: The Civil War Writings of De Forest and Bierce.* Knoxville: University of Tennessee Press, 1997.

Scott, Robert N., and Henry M. Lazelle. *The War of the Rebellion: A Compilation of the Official Records of the Union and Confederate Armies.* Series 1, vol. XXIII, pt. 1. Washington, DC: U.S. Government Printing Office, 1889.

Scribner, Theodore T. *Indiana's Roll of Honor.* Vol. II. Indianapolis: Straight, 1866.

Sistler, Byron, and Barbara Sistler. *1890 Civil War Veterans Census, Tennessee.* Evanston, IL: Byron Sistler, 1978.

Solomon, Eric. "The Bitterness of Battle: Ambrose Bierce's War Fiction." *Midwest Quarterly* 5 (1964): 147–65 Rpt. in *Critical Essays on Ambrose Bierce.* Ed. Cathy N. Davidson. Boston: Hall, 1982. 182–94.

Stallman, R. W. *Stephen Crane: A Biography.* New York: Braziller, 1968.

Stallman, R. W., and Lillian Gilkes, ed. *Stephen Crane: Letters.* New York: New York University Press, 1960.

Starling, L. Letter to Brigadier General Hazen. 15 October 1863. Papers of Ambrose Bierce. University of Virginia Lib., Charlottesville, VA.

Stevenson, David. *Indiana's Roll of Honor.* Vol. I. Indianapolis: Straight, 1864.

Sword, Wiley. *Embrace an Angry Wind: The Confederacy's Last Hurrah; Spring Hill, Franklin, and Nashville.* New York: Harper, 1992.

Tennessee Civil War Centennial Commission. *Tennesseans in the Civil War: A Military History of Confederate and Union Rosters with Available Rosters of Personnel.* Part II. Nashville: Civil War Centennial Commission, 1965.

Thornbrough, Emma Lou. *Indiana in the Civil War Era: 1850–1880.* Indianapolis: Indiana Historical Society, 1995.

Tucker, Glenn. *Chickamauga: Bloody Battle in the West.* New York: Bobbs-Merrill, 1961.

Turner, George Edward. *Victory Rode the Rails: The Strategic Place of the Railroads in the Civil War.* Lincoln: University of Nebraska Press, 1992.

United States. Dept. of Defense. Army Center of Military History. *American Military History.* Washington, DC: U.S. Government Printing Office, 1988.

———. Dept. of Interior. Geological Survey. Map of Calhoun North, Georgia. 1: 24,000 scale. 1972.

———. ———. Tennessee Valley Authority. Topographic maps of Athens, Elkmont, Huntsville, Maysville, Meridianville, and Tannner, Alabama. 1:24,0000 scale. 1938–58.

———. Dept. of War. *Atlas to Accompany the Official Records of the Union and Confederate Armies.* 1891–1895. Reprinted with an introduction by Richard Sommers as *The Official Military Atlas of the Civil War.* New York: Random, 1983.

———. ———. *The War of the Rebellion: A Compilation of the Official Records of the Union and Confederate Armies.* Washington, DC: U.S. Government Printing Office, 1880–1901.

Van Horne, Thomas B. *History of the Army of the Cumberland.* Vol. II. Cincinnati: Clarke, 1876.

Villard, Henry. *Memoirs of Henry Villard, Journalist and Financier, 1835–1900.* Vol. II, *1863–1900.* Boston: Houghton, 1904.

"We have been shown a letter." *Elkhart Review.* 21 Feb. 1863.

Wharton, Edith. "Writing a War Story." *The Collected Short Stories of Edith Wharton.* Vol. 2. Ed. R. W. B. Lewis. New York: Scribners, 1969.

Williams, Stanley T. Introduction. *A Volunteer's Adventures: A Union Captain's Record of the Civil War.* By John William De Forest. New York: Rhinehart, 1946.

Wilson, Edmond. *Patriotic Gore: Studies in the Literature of the American Civil War.* 1962. Boston: Northeastern University Press, 1984.

Wilt, Napier. "Ambrose Bierce and the Civil War." *American Literature* 1 (1929): 260–85.

Woodruff, Stuart. *The Short Stories of Ambrose Bierce: A Study in Polarity.* Pittsburgh: University of Pittsburgh Press, 1964.

Yates, Bowling C. *Historical Guide for Kennesaw Mountain National Battlefield Park and Marietta, Georgia.* Marietta, GA: Kennesaw Mountain Historical Association, 1976.

Index

Page numbers in **boldface** refer to maps.

Davis, Sam, 39, 75
De Forest, John William, ix, 136–39, 141, 144
"Death and the Child" (Crane), 140
Decatur, Ala., **50**–52
Deerslayer, The (Cooper), 132
Devil's Dictionary, The (Bierce), ix, 21, 39, 57, 74, 100, 105
Devil's Lexicographer, The (Fatout), 6, 120
Dodge, General Greenville, 75
Dorman-Smith, Edward Eric, 7
Drum Taps (Whitman), ix
Druse, Carter, 28–29, 31–33, 37, 53, 81, 88
Dudley, Lieutenant Will, 40–41
Duncan, Russell, 3

E
"Editha" (Howells), 140–41
Edwards, Jonathan, 36
Elkhart (town), Ind., **4**, 9, 31, 35, 42
Elkhart County, Ind., 42
Elkhart Review, The (newspaper), 44, 55
Elkmont, Ala., **50**, 52
England, 13, 68, 74, 125

F
Farquhar, Peyton, 48, 51–55, 75, 82, 92–93, 115, 127
Fatout, Paul, 10, 116, 120, 122
Fetterley, Judith, 135–36, 140
Fiend's Delight, The (Bierce, Grile), 99
First World War (*see* World War I)
Fisher, Philip, 135–36
Fleming, Henry, 24, 136, 143
Forrest, General Nathan Bedford, 51–52, 89
Fort Benning, Ga., 7
Fort Donelson, Tenn., 100

Fort Henry, Tenn., 100
"Four Days in Dixie" (Bierce), 52–53, 113–14, 119
Franco-Prussian War, 15
Fredericksburg, Va., 139
Fussell, Paul, 134, 150

G
Gatewood, Jeff, 54
Genesis, 25, 27
"George Thurston: Three Incidents in the Life of a Man" (Bierce), 10, 19, 58, 60, 113–14, 118, 122, 125–26
Gilgamesh, ix
Glenn, Eliza, 96–97
Going After Cacciato (O'Brien), x
Goose Creek, Ind., 8
Graffenreid, Anderton, 91–93
Grafton, W.Va., **4**, 9, 23, **27**, 31, 66–67, 71
Grant, Ulysses Simpson, 15, 40–41, 46, 100–101, 103
Grayrock, Private William, 33–35, 37, 81
Great War and Modern Memory, The (Fussell), 134
Greenbrier River, W.Va., 9, 26, 55
Greene, Bennett Story, 40–41, 76
Grenander, Mary, 3, 32, 73
Grile, Dod (Bierce pseudonym), 99

H
Hackworth, Lieutenant David, 39
Halcrow, Major Creede, 45–46
Halcrow, Sergeant Caffal, 42–43
Hale, Nathan, 75
Hamilton County, Tenn., 79
Hard Facts: Setting and Form in the American Novel (Fisher), 135
Harte, Bret, 13, 137
Hartroy, Captain Parrol, 66–68, 70–71, 81

The Devil's Topographer was designed and typeset on a Macintosh computer system using QuarkXPress software. The body text is set in 9.75/13 ITC Galliard and display type is set in Ellington. This book was designed and typeset by Kelly Gray and manufactured by Thomson-Shore, Inc.